# How To Win Like The Banks - Winning Forex Trading Strategies 2021

*Learn How to Multiply Your Money Using These Simple Proven Strategies That the Banks Use. Earn Passive Income With Simple Trading Strategies and Learn How to Make Money in Minutes and Sometimes Seconds!!*

**Terrence Bailey**

# Table of Contents

# Introduction

Choosing a financial market to trade is always a tough choice for a beginner. Many wannabe traders started their trading journey with the stock market because it is both popular and easy to start with. Both knowledge and resources are available in excess for the stock market, and this makes beginners interested in investing try out their luck in the open stock market.

If an amateur is asked about the largest financial market in the world, they would say that it is the stock market. The stock market receives a lot of press and social media attention, making it popular among financial illiterates. However, despite its popularity, the stock market is not the largest financial market in the world. The largest financial market in the world is the forex market, which had a daily trading volume of close to 6 trillion US dollars in 2020. Foreign exchange trading can be a hard trading style to get into because of its overwhelming nature. Since it is hard for beginners to grasp the underlying concepts, we have written this book in an easy language.

## Why Have We Written This Book?

There are many resources in the market about forex trading, but only a few teach the basics critical for a beginner. Most of the popular books that teach forex trading are hard to be understood by an absolute beginner. When writing this book, the author made sure that the writing would be easy and understandable for readers to consume the provided knowledge. The primary focus is to teach forex trading easily for forex enthusiasts.

## How to Read This Book

An absolute beginner who does not know the forex market can start the book from the first chapter. If you are an advanced trader, we recommend starting the book from chapter 5 for better results.

Ensure that you use cognitive techniques such as mind maps and the Feynman technique to grasp as much as possible from this book.

# Understanding Financial Independence

Most people have day-to-day jobs and have savings stored in their bank to retire with a good chunk of money. However, we can achieve financial independence only when we can increase our savings. Many Americans in the 21st century understand the importance of financial independence and try out their luck in the open markets as investors and traders.

### What is an Investment?

An investment is a situation where you invest your money in a particular asset and expect it to grow in value. Therefore, we can usually consider the investment as a long-term way to increase your savings.

### What is Trading?

Trading is a financial concept where investors try to bet the market in the short term to gain profits of their own. Trading is complex, stressful, and can be called a roller coaster ride of emotions.

# Different Financial Markets

Before diving into the world of forex trading, you must know about different financial markets that can affect the forex market.

## *Stock Market*

In the stock market, companies provide a part of their company as shares. When an investor buys shares of a stock, he becomes one of the many rightful owners of that stock. The stock market can affect the economy and is in the news often. We can use the stock market for both investing and trading. Different exchanges such as the New York Stock Exchange (or NYSE) centralize and control the stock market all around the world. Both governments and central banks support the stock market and sometimes even bail out companies from huge losses.

Many individuals consider long-term stock investing more reliable because it is safe and can guarantee you returns for most of the time. However, stock trading that happens in the short term is difficult, and it is very hard for retail traders to win the game because the market is unpredictable. Despite these reasons, traders love the excitement that comes with the stock market.

Both the stock market and forex market depend on each other. A bad stock market crash can affect currency exchange prices and vice versa. Apple, Google, Amazon, and Tesla are some of the popular public trading companies in the U.S. stock market.

## *Cryptocurrency Market*

The cryptocurrency market is always in the news because of its sheer profitability and controversies. The cryptocurrency market is decentralized and runs on blockchain technology, the latter of which is both reliable and safe. Over the last ten years, the cryptocurrency market has provided considerable returns to investors and has much potential in the future. Bitcoin, Ethereum, Litecoin, Cardano, and XRP are some of the popular cryptocurrencies.

However, the cryptocurrency market is volatile and can crash for no specific reason. The forex market is not affected by fluctuations in the cryptocurrency market.

## *Derivatives Market*

Derivatives are financial markets where traders both speculate and bet on the market movements. Popular derivatives are options, futures, and forwards. An investor needs to be aware of the fundamentals that influence the markets they are betting upon to participate in a derivative market. Derivatives are often different types, and each needs a different strategy to succeed.

You can use derivatives in forex trading. Investors use both options and futures to bet both long and short positions. However, derivative markets in the forex market are not as aggressive as the stock market.

## *Forex Market*

The forex market is used to exchange currencies with a rate that is known as an exchange rate. Therefore, forex markets have a massive influence on the country's economy and affect people's lives when the currency value decreases.

This book will discuss the forex market and different trading strategies and philosophies to help a retail investor. However, to trade, you need to be first aware of some common details that successful traders recommend.

### Things to Be Aware Of Before Starting Trading in the Forex Market

Before entering the forex market, you should create a checklist and judge whether you are ready for the market. Making a quick reality check can help you avoid ways that lead to financial debts, which can devastate your professional and personal career. Introspecting the answers that you have given to this checklist can help you realize your current financial freedom that is essential for a forex trader.

Checklist:

Please take a paper and pen and answer the below-mentioned questions:

- Do you have any debts?

- Are your savings good?

- Do you plan on making any big financial decisions and need money for them?

- Are you interested in trading, or are you just doing it because everyone else is doing it?

- Are you comfortable with a computer and have sufficient skills to operate a trading platform?

- What do you expect from trading?

- Where are you looking at yourself within the next ten years?

Answering these questions to yourself can make you realize whether or not you are ready to experiment with the forex market.

## Six Essential Skills for Traders

Before talking about forex trading, it is our responsibility to let you know some fundamental skills that traders, irrespective of the financial route they have to master.

1. **Analytical skill:** Traders often stumble with charts, technical indicators, and averages that need a good grasp of mathematics. Of course, nowadays, there is countless software that does this work for you. Nevertheless, having a good analytical skill set can help a trader. To increase your analytical skills, we recommend you solve puzzles such as Sudoku.

2. **Love for research:** A trader needs to research a lot. Researching is hard, and often people need to collect hundreds of notes to consume data and make their point. Make sure you use research tools such as mind maps, flow charts, and digital software for researching the content that is essential for your trade.

3. **Focus:** This is a hard skill to master. Traders often deviate from their plan due to a fear of missing out on the trades that are happening. While it is good to get some profits, a lack of focus will always result in confusion and frustration. Make a rational plan and try to focus on it most of the time.

4. **Control:** Control is the ultimate way to make sure that you are ready to trade. We are humans, and humans are bundled with emotions that can burst out when there is a problem. As a trader, you need to control these emotions and focus on your plan.

5. **Journaling:** There is nothing better than self-evaluation for a trader, so spend some time writing a journal for your trade. Mention how you feel about the trade and stick down all the charts or reports that helped you succeed in the trade.

6. **Time management:** For any profession, managing your time is important. As a trader, make sure that you make your To-do list every day before starting the trade. Use techniques such as the Pomodoro Technique not to waste your time procrastinating during research.

We have provided a ton of information about forex trading, strategies, and trading philosophies in this book, and we hope you enjoy reading this book as much as we enjoyed writing it.

## Disclaimer:

All the details in this book are only for your educational purpose. The author of the book is in no way responsible for your trading decisions. Make sure you do Trading with only the money you can afford to lose. If you are still unaware, please contact a professional advisor regarding your trades.

# Chapter 1: Basics of Forex Trading

Forex trading is the largest financial market in the world. According to the Bank for International Settlements (BIS), more than 6 trillion USD trade happens on a single forex trading day, much larger than the daily volume of stock markets or the latest booming cryptocurrency market. Most of the time when we talk about forex trading, we will be referring to spot FX trading, where the trades will settle approximately within one or two days. FX trading can also be done using both futures and forwards, where the trades will be settled on a future date. This book will primarily discuss spot FX trading, which is popular and relevant to a retail trader.

Traders of any financial instrument skim through the basics and prefer advanced topics such as fundamental and technical analysis. With overwhelming information and techniques available, the trader may lose his patience and won't remember the basics that make the forex market function. Understanding basics and revisiting them constantly is a successful forex trader's secret.

## What is Foreign Exchange Trading?

Foreign exchange trading stands for the exchange of currencies. All these exchanges happen in a decentralized international market known as the forex market. When you exchange currencies in a forex market, you are buying and lending a currency simultaneously. This is the reason why currencies are traded in pairs.

*A Real-Life Example*

Let us suppose that you visited Japan from the United States for a month's vacation. When you leave the United States, you will have domestic currency (USD) with you. Furthermore, when you reach the airport in Tokyo, you can exchange your domestic currency for foreign currency (JPY), which can be used during your stay in Japan.

Let us suppose that the exchange rate is JPY USD 100. That is, for every one USD, you will receive 100 JPY. If you have 1,000 USD, you will get 100,000 JPY which you can use for your vacation.

After a month, you return home and have decided to convert your remaining JPY into USD to use in the United States. You have a remaining amount of 10,000 JPY and for the previous rate you would have received 100 USD. However, the exchange rate has changed to 95 JPY, and thus you will receive only 95 in USD.

The JPY has increased its value in the previous example, and the USD has decreased its value. If the exchange rate has increased to 105 JPY, JPY has decreased its value and USD has increased its value.

# How Did Forex Trading Emerge?

Banks started to use currencies as a monetary system because the previously accepted gold standard system was inflexible and impractical. When the gold standard was in force, the U.S. government controlled the entire gold reserves in order to manage the financial model of the country effectively. After WWII, inflation decreased and the economy started to boom all around the world. In the next few years, the world saw revolutionary monetary changes that lead to a fiat currency system and flexible currency trading, which is now famously known as the Forex market, where forex stands for foreign exchange.

# How Big Is the Forex Market?

Even though it is relatively new compared to the worldwide stock markets, the Forex market is the market with the highest daily trade volume. For example, the forex market controls approximately 6 Trillion USD a day compared to the 230 billion USD of the NYSE stock market.

# Trading Forex Using Currency Pairs

When you buy a stock or a cryptocurrency, you will usually buy the asset and own them until you decide to sell them for a profit or loss. Forex trading uses currency pairs to trade in the market. When you buy or sell a currency pair, you expect to hold a specific currency by lending others.

# A Brief History of Currency and Forex Trading

For centuries humans have improved their ability to make trade and exchange goods with the help of different currency systems.

Close to 6000 years ago, humans used to follow the barter system as a traditional currency system. In a barter system, an individual exchanges an item to possess their desired item. For example, if a farmer needs to sell their milk, he visits a provisionary or stationery store to exchange milk with one of their items. While the barter system worked for small provinces, it became complicated as the population started to grow.

The inefficiency of the barter system led people to start using a standard exchange system dominated by both gold and silver. Over time, both banks and monetary institutions chose gold as an efficient item for exchange as it was and is both scarce and difficult to harvest. Other alternative systems such as paper bills have hit the world but have not been implemented effectively by several countries.

In the 1600s, humans started to use currency notes for daily use. People started to adopt currencies for all kinds of transactions within very little time as it is more comfortable and trustworthy. Unfortunately, governments started to print their own currencies and this made foreign transactions unreliable. However, after many problems and discussions, economists and governments worldwide decided to use USD as the reserved currency for foreign transactions. Everything worked well until the United States ran out of gold reserves and officially announced that it could no longer implement the gold standard system.

After a few years, the forex trading platform was introduced to make foreign transactions work efficiently, and since then, currency trading has grown exponentially.

# Basics Of Forex Trading

Forex traders must understand the basics of the forex market before they start trading. In this section, some of the important characteristics and details of the forex market are presented.

## *What Is Spot Trading?*

In a forex market, the transactions (or currencies) are usually done as spot transactions. Trading in the forex market only happens in pairs, and so when you make a spot trade, you are buying one currency and selling another one. All the spot transactions that are placed in the forex market are usually settled within two working days.

## *How Are Currencies Traded?*

In the forex market, we can trade currencies only in pairs. The first currency is known as the base currency, and you are buying it by betting on the secondary currency, which is technically known as counter or quote currency. All these currency pairs are traded with a quote.

Let us explain this to you with a simple example. If you are holding a position of USD/EUR, then it means that you are betting that the U.S. dollar will do better than the EUR.

Here USD is the base currency, and EUR is the secondary currency. Let suppose that at the time you bought USD/EUR; the quote is USD/EUR 0.8. It says that you can buy 0.8 EUR for 1 USD. If the quote changes from 0.8 to 0.9, EUR is weakening, and the dollar is moving stronger. In the same way, if the quote changes from 0.8 to 0.7, it means that the EUR is going stronger and USD is becoming weaker.

All the currencies in the forex market are usually abbreviated and are represented using pairs.

Here are some of the examples:

USD/JPY—USD stands for U.S. Dollar, and JPY stands for Japanese Yen

AUD/CAD—AUD stand for Australian Dollar, and CAD stands for Canadian Dollar

EUR/GBP—EUR stands for Euro and GBP stands for British Pound

EUR/CHF—EUR stands for Euro, and CHF stands for the Swiss franc

We will be talking about some of these popular currency pairs in the later chapters of this book.

USD is often called the base currency as it is roughly involved in 80% of the currency trades that occur in the market. All the trades that do not involve USD are known as cross trades and are usually difficult to liquidate as fewer speculators are betting on them. The most popular currency pairs in the market are known as majors, and they all involve USD.

### *What Are Pips, and Why Are They Essential?*

Usually in the forex market, currencies are traded up to four decimal points. Any change in this decimal number can impact the market. According to Forex terminology, these decimal points are called pips. Almost all traders and trading platforms provide their spread value for currency pairs using pips. Each currency is expressed in different pips. Before starting a trade, we recommend finding out how pips are expressed for your currency pairs to avoid confusion.

For example, the Japanese Yen is calculated only to two decimal points. Thus, if the price of Yen moves from 165.23 to 165.29, then it is expressed as six pips.Here,the difference between exchange prices is six which a trader can use to represent in pips.

### *What is Bid/Ask Price in a Forex Market?*

You might have already observed a Bid/Ask price terminology if you had a foreign vacation and had to exchange your regular currency for the foreign currency.

When you look at a foreign exchange trade, you will see both bids and asks for a currency pair. You will use bid rate if you are looking to buy a currency pair and offer rate if you are looking to sell a currency. Fundamentally the difference between Bid/Ask price is known as a spread.

Whenever you use a forex currency pair to represent their exchange rates, it is important to use the abbreviation. For example, USD is an abbreviation for the United States dollar. We recommend using the currency symbol notation (for example the U.S. would be $) on every other occasion, such as while mentioning the capital or deposited amount in your trading account or calculating your profits and losses.

### *Understanding How to Trade*

Usually, brokers provide different options according to the margin amount you have in your trading account. However, forex traders are usually given an option to hold either a mini lot or a lot according to their credit score. When you own a lot, you need to provide a standardized margin amount of 1,000 USD, which can be used to bet the market with a leverage option of 100:1. This will make you control 100,000 USD of trade. On the other hand, mini lots will ask you to provide a 100 USD margin amount for controlling the 10,000 USD base price in the market.

To understand more about the characteristics of forex trading, you need to be aware of certain basic tools that are essential.

## Basic Tools of Forex Trading

To trade in any forex market, you need to either long or short your position. When you take a long position, you are buying the currency; whereas when you take a short position, you are selling the currency. No matter whether it is a long or short position, your transactions usually happen in orders. However, they can be executed in different ways according to your preference.

### *Order Types in the Forex Market*

### Market Order

Usually, when you look at a forex chart in your trading platform, you will see a price. You can immediately execute it and trade it according to the numbers you see. This type of trade is called a market order. However, it needs to be mentioned that as the forex market is involved with many other players, you technically cannot buy or sell your orders at the price you saw. Therefore, even though not accurate, market orders are always the most common way to execute a trade in the forex market.

## Limit Order

Limit orders are introduced to avoid the flaws that market orders provide. When you place a limit order, you will have an option to enter the price you are unwilling to cross while executing the trade. A limit order can be applied both during the buy and sell of the currencies.

For example, let us suppose that you are willing to buy EUR at 0.9 but cannot buy it if it rises above 0.9. So, now you place a limit order, and your transaction will be processed only if the EUR price is still 0.9 or below.

Limit orders are life-saving, especially if you are a day trader and have many other trades to participate in.

## Stop Orders

Stop orders are essential for any trader irrespective of the financial market because they can help you protect your profits and stop losses that you cannot afford.

When you place a stop order, you will be asked to provide a value where the system can trigger a trade for you. Thus, you can use both stop losses and gain profits to execute stop orders.

For example, suppose you make a USD/EUR trade at 0.8 and hit it to 0.7 to gain some profits. However, you do not want to lose more than the limit of 0.9. So you place a stop-loss order at 0.9, and if the currency reaches 0.9, your order will be executed.

### *Why Are Stop Orders Inconvenient Sometimes?*

While stop orders are great, they can be entirely frustrating during a busy trading day because your orders will depend entirely on market makers. Stop orders can also make you lose your profits during a highly volatile day when the prices fluctuate.

For this reason, brokers have provided other alternatives for traders who cannot effectively use stop orders. However, remember that these strategies can cost you more commissions.

## Order Cancels Other

Order cancels other (OCO) orders are used by traders who are focusing mainly on the support/resistance levels of the market. During this phase, when both bears and bulls are aggressively selling and buying the pairs, there is a chance for the market to move otherwise.

Due to this reason, traders use OCO to create two limit or stop orders. Then, when the price reaches either, the order will be executed, and the other one will be automatically removed.

## Stop-Limit Order

Traders use this order when they know the market will move in their anticipated way but are worried about the intensity of the move. So, they place a limit and stop orders not to exceed their limit. If the market moves too fast, the stop order will be triggered. Stop-limit orders are sometimes frustrating because they can end your trades prematurely, making you not gain those profits which you could have otherwise.

### *Understanding Rollovers as a Forex Trader*

Usually, when an investor buys a forex pair in the spot market, he is asked to settle the trade within two days. Therefore, if you have an open position in these two days, you need to use rollovers to hold the open position indefinitely.

Rollovers are necessary because no one wants to hold foreign currency in their trading bank accounts. It may lead to confusion and, practically, is not a good way to handle your trades. Rollovers offer interests that you will either be paid or which you need to pay for your open positions. If you are not interested in paying for rollovers, you need to close your trades within 5 p.m. EST.

## Why are Rollover Times at 5 p.m. EST?

All the rollovers are reset at 5 p.m. EST because it is the start of the international forex market day in Singapore. Therefore, every day you need to settle your trades within this time or be charged interest for your positions.

If it is a weekend, then you will get a three-day holding period. All the rollover interest rates will constantly change according to the interest rates of primary and secondary currencies in the trade. Nowadays, all retail trading platforms automatically use the rollover methodology in order to make the trading account not control the open positions capital.

## How to Understand the Rollover Charge

Rollover charges are entirely dependent on the type of currency you have chosen. When you participate in a spot forex trade, you borrow a base currency by lending the secondary currency to the market players.

For example, let us use GBP/USD. If you participate in spot trade, you are lending GBP by borrowing USD to the market players. So during the rollover time, when you have GBP in your bank account, you will be provided interest by the Bank of England, and because you have borrowed USD, you will be paying interest rate to the U.S. federal bank.

If you are a short trader, you need not worry about rollover charges because your trades will settle within the same trading day. The difference between interest rates can lead to a passive income. For example, holding a GBP/USD pair with a 4% interest of GBP and a 2% interest rate of USD can help you receive 2 percent as profit.

However, it would be best to do complete research according to your currency pairs before starting a trade. Many individual clearing firms have their own regulations and follow their own set of rules.

# Advantages of Forex Trading

Being a financial market with a higher day cap than any other, forex trading is incredibly liquid and has a lot in store for a regular day trader. This section will argue why forex trading is better than the other financial routes such as stock markets or cryptocurrency.

### It Is Open for 24 Hours

The forex market is open 24 hours for six days, and this is an easy way to trade for everyone around the world. Nevertheless, foreign investors usually need to be aware of different time zones and approach the one they like best.

### Liquidity Is Not a Problem

Liquidity is the ability to turn your open positions into fiat currency whenever possible. There is no problem with liquidity for traders who are trading the major currency pairs in the forex market. Moreover, all the brokerage firms can instantly confirm your transactions due to the liquidity.

### *Transaction Costs Are Very Low*

All the transaction costs in forex trades are significantly lower when compared to stock markets, because forex brokerage firms collect a spread instead of charging a high commission fee for the trade.

### *You Can Use the Leverage*

Leverage can help you to borrow money with a small margin amount. Leverage is wonderful because it can give you financial independence to deal with money you do not own. However, leverage needs to be understood thoroughly by a forex trader as it is sometimes complex and dangerous.

## Disadvantages of Forex Trading

Like any other financial market, the Forex Market has its own set of disadvantages.

### *It is Less Transparent*

Unlike stock markets, the forex market is not centralized, and this makes the traders entirely dependent on brokers for the prices. This is the reason why forex charts change according to the broker.

### *Hard to Learn*

Unlike traditional stock markets, learning about the forex market is difficult, and it is hard to find valid information about different indicators and patterns that can help you win the trade. Therefore, a lot of learning curve is needed for making profits.

Your trading account can be reduced in funds if there is a change in the currencies' interest rate. Also, rollover charges can be increased during the settlement period due to this.

# Forex Market Timings

Forex market trading is not done at one central location, but it happens between different participants worldwide using phone and electronic communication networks(ECNs). The advantage of this practice is that the trade happens five days a week.

The market usually starts at 5 P.M EST on Sunday and ends at 4 P.M EST on Friday. The reason why traders followed this practice is because of central banks. Central banks rely on forex transactions and since the floating currency is necessary for foreign transactions, running the markets according to their time zones is essential. The demand for foreign currency transactions has made the forex market adopt 24 hours per day rules.

The forex trading day kick starts with a Singapore and Australian Session and will be followed by Tokyo and London Sessions. The forex trading day finally ends with the New York session. Usually, the market is busy during London and New York sessions as USD and EUR are the most important currencies in the forex market.

# Difference Between Stock and Forex Markets

Stock markets consist of publicly traded companies that want to raise capital for their production and infrastructure costs. All of the publicly traded companies in the market are liable to share their trade reports with the public. Stock markets have a significant impact on the economy, but they cannot affect the economy directly unless the whole stock market crashes, like during the Dot-Com burst in the 90s.

On the other hand, the forex market deals with the currency that citizens usually use to purchase goods or any other services within a country. Therefore, a change in exchange price can directly affect a country's social, political, and economic conditions. Due to its absolute power and impact on a country's economy, governments try to hold absolute control over currency and take absolute measures to stabilize their exchange rate against foreign currencies.

### *Why Do Governments Want to Control Foreign Exchange Rates?*

As said before, a drastic change in the exchange rate of a currency due to a bad economy can change citizens' social life in a country. A decrease in exchange rates directly means that the economy is on the verge of collapse. Governments do not want their economies to collapse, so they understand the importance of forex exchange rates for trade balance and domestic development.

Let us take, for example, China. China is now one of the superpowers globally and indirectly in a trade war with the United States. Over the last 50 years, China has gone through radical reforms and introduced capitalistic reforms in a monitored society.

China understands the importance of currency rates and wants to have ultimate control over them. That is why it has set a fixed conversion rate of 1 USD to 7.27 yuan. This gives China ultimate control, who believe that it is a better way to control its international trade instead of appreciating its rate with the U.S. dollar. These fixed currencies are known as peg currencies, and many economists debate whether or not it is a better way to secure economic growth.

As a forex trader, you need to understand that developing or underdeveloped governments can sometimes take absolute measures to manipulate the exchange rates of currencies by converting their foreign reserves or by allowing high taxation rates for imports. Countries like Venezuela and Zimbabwe have made these mistakes before and have ruined their economies.

# Chapter 2: The Mechanics Of Forex Market

The foreign exchange market depends on various market players and regulators to effectively monitor trades and keep the system alive. Therefore, learning about important market players, regulators, and different trading strategies is essential for understanding the mechanics of the forex market. In addition, understanding these concepts can help you to execute trades with much more confidence.

## Who Are the Players in the Forex Market?

Understanding different forex players in the market and knowing how they balance the forex market is important for every forex trader. Online trading has changed the operational policies of foreign traders over the years. We are now mentioning the markets regarding volume.

### Private Banks

Banks are the biggest participants in the forex market. Both commercial and investment banks participate in the forex market to neutralize their risks and effectively manage their clients' funds.

All banks have a dealing desk to control the funds by following a risk management strategy that involves hedging and derivatives usage. Usually, banks handle forex trades in more than 50 million parcels and significantly impact exchange rates when liquidating their positions.

### Central Banks

Central banks control the monetary policies of the economy in a country. Countries usually have reserves and foreign currencies to facilitate trade transactions. The reserved currency can be used to deal with foreign debts, relations and services. The central bank also participates in the forex market to stabilize the currency's value as the exchange rates directly impact the economy.

### *Multinational Companies*

Also known as commercial traders, businesses and corporations use the forex market to transfer their foreign revenues to the domestic currency. Multinational companies use various strategies to either gain interest or reduce transaction costs.

### *Speculators*

Speculators are the forex market players who trade in the forex markets without any purpose but to gain profits. Big players such as hedge funds and retail traders fall under this category. Speculators follow both fundamental and technical analysis to predict market movement and will utilize these indicators to make a profit.

### *Brokerage Firms*

These are the participants in the forex market who act as a mediator between the market participants. As a result, they get a part of the spread or a commission for every transaction.

## Forex Regulators

The forex market is decentralized, and no one ultimately regulates or controls it as a whole. However, each country has its central authorities to regulate its currencies. Knowing about these forex regulators and how they function is important for a forex trader.

### SFBC

The Swiss Federal Banking Commission (or SFBC) has the ultimate control over the monitoring of the Swiss Franc and has complete authority to maintain and stabilize the Swiss economic system. However, it does not have authority over its banking system as the Swiss government has given privileged authority to banks. This exclusive privilege is why the Swiss franc is considered a haven by foreign investors and is thus responsible for an enormous number of offshore accounts in the Swiss Banks.

### IDAC

The International Depository Authority of Canada (or IDAC) has the control of regulating the Canadian economy. It is a self-regulatory organization and follows various measures to strengthen the exchange rate of the Canadian dollar.

### Federal Bank

The United States, on the other hand, uses the Federal Reserve Bank to control and create monetary policies that can strengthen the U.S. dollar. As the U.S. dollar is a reserve currency for more than 40% of the foreign investors, the Federal Bank makes separate rules for offshore accounts. Organizations such as Commodity Futures Trading Commission (CFTC), Over The Counter (OTC), and Commodity Exchange Act (CEA) collaborate with the Fed to assure that the USD won't fall under any anti-fraud and anti-manipulation.

We suggest you skim through the monetary organizations of the currency pairs you are trading with before participating in a forex trade.

## Understanding Leverage as a Forex Trader

Leverage is an excellent tool for investors because it allows them to trade a far larger amount than they own. This choice of lending large amounts of money for a forex trader cannot be ignored.

When brokerage firms provide leverage options for your trading account, they will ask you to deposit a small amount of money known as a margin. Usually, a lot in the forex trading platforms means $1,000. So with a margin of $1,000, you can get $100,000 leverage. That is a 100:1 leverage ratio. Even though 100:1 is the recommended leverage ratio for forex brokerage firms, many firms now offer close to 400:1 leverage options for their traders due to competition.

### What Is the Problem With Leverage?

While leverages help you to control more money than you have, they also mean that you can lose your money faster. Thus, over-leverage is often harmful to a forex investor's peace of mind and psychological strength. Also, almost no financial markets provide leverage as forex brokers provide. This is because the liquidation of currencies is easy and also because the forex market is decentralized. However, many forex firms give false claims to traders to make themselves profitable by occasional costs in the form of spreads.

### What Is the Initial Margin?

The money you need to deposit in the trading account to utilize leverage options initially is the initial margin. It is usually $1,000 for retail traders.

### What Is A Margin Call?

When the trader has open positions bought using the leverage money, the broker will have the right to either sell the shares or hold them if you lose your margin amount even before closing the trade. When your account reaches below the minimum balance, you need to deposit the money known as margin call to resume forex trading. Usually, brokers provide close to two days to deposit your margin call amount in the trading account.

*Relation Between Leverage and Commissions*

Many beginners believe that the forex brokers follow a no-commission rule. However, it is not true because forex traders charge commissions in spreads when quoting the Bid/Ask price. Forex brokers provide leverage options to increase the number of trades a forex trader does in order to earn commissions. If you are serious about forex trading, we suggest finding brokers that charge flat commissions and tighter spreads.

# Derivatives in the Forex Market

Forex trading is mostly about spot trading, where traders exchange currencies, and exchanges will settle the trade within two days. Spot trading should be your way to the forex market if you are a beginner. Apart from spot forex trading, the market also provides investors to trade with derivatives, just like in the stock market. Some of the popular derivatives in the forex market are forwards, futures, options, and swaps. Learning about derivatives and their mechanics is essential even if you are not interested in trading with them because they move and affect the market.

*Who Are the Different Players in the Market?*

It is strange to believe, but most of the transactions that take place in the market are entirely speculative. Speculators trade currency pairs for only one reason, which is to gain profit. The other important players in the market are hedging their positions for different reasons. Financial institutions such as private banks, insurance companies, and multinational companies with foreign revenue fall under the second category.

Most of these players use the spot market to trade their currency pairs. However, not all are interested in spot trading, and so the forex market provides a chance for investors to use derivatives. As a result, approximately 1 trillion USD of the daily 6 trillion USD forex market is occupied by the derivatives.

It is entirely dependent on the participant to choose what derivative they want to use. Usually, a forex participant chooses a derivative based on his purpose.

## Understanding Forwards

Forwards are used to lock a specific currency transaction for a future date. Normally, investors use forwards to take advantage of the interest rates provided by central banks for holding the positions. Forwards are unregulated and can sometimes cause problems, especially while trying to liquidate the contracts.

For example, let us suppose that CAD provides a 3% interest rate for the positions and USD offers 1% interest rate. So now the investor converts his currency into CAD to get more interest. However, he will buy a forward contract and will lock the transaction to happen at a particular time. Thus, investors can make profits as long as the interest rates don't change drastically.

The only problem with forwards is that the contract prices will increase when there is a demand and decrease when there is no demand. These prices are called premium and discount.

## Understanding Futures

Futures follow the same concept as forwards but are regulated. Futures are regulated and have speculators who are constantly betting upon different currencies and commodities. Futures in markets are not new. They are created to help businesses deal with future results by buying a contract from the speculators who are sure that the future result will be on their way.

For example, let us suppose that a farmer is interested in growing mangoes. However, he is not sure whether or not the price of mangoes will be the same next year. So he buys a futures contract to buy his crop at a fixed price for a hefty premium known as a futures contract. This future contract is usually provided by a speculator who believes that the price of mangoes is not going to fall. So, he sells the futures contract and is obligated to buy the mangoes at that specific price.

In the forex market, speculators can sell future contracts for currency pairs. However, trading with futures can be complex and risky if you are completely unaware of the mechanics behind it. Also, many brokerage firms will only allow you to trade in futures contracts if you provide them a margin or a bond.

*Understanding Options*

Options are the most popular of the derivative markets because they cost less to trade. Options provide a choice to whether or not to exercise your contract, unlike futures or forwards where the contract owner is obligated to the contract. Options are used to bet the currency pair price movement in the forex market for a future date. Options contracts have an expiry date after which they are worthless.

## How Do Options Work?

Options are used to bet whether the price of a currency pair will be either up or down within a particular time frame. There are two types of options—call and put.

## What Is A Call Option?

When you buy a call option contract, you fundamentally believe that the currency's price will go up with a particular date. Therefore, you pay a premium to buy a set of currency for a fixed price within a specific date. Remember that the owner of the call options contract is not obligated to exercise his right. In contrast, the seller of the options contract is obligated to provide him with the currency if the owner exercises his right.

## What Is A Put Option?

When you buy a put option, you are betting with the market that the currency's price will go down. You pay a premium to sell your position for a fixed price within a particular date. If you are right, then you will exercise the options contract to sell your positions. You, however, don't have any obligation, whereas the put options contract seller is obligated to buy your currency at a strike price.

The premium of the options contracts depends on the demand for the contract, strike price, and expiry date.

## Why are Options Used?

Options are usually used by financial instructions, banks and retail investors as a risk management strategy. By hedging your position, you can minimize your losses and can exit an unsuccessful trade with a small profit on your hand. In addition, investors use various options strategies such as spreads to manage their portfolios effectively.

## How Are Options Traded in the Forex Market?

Even though the fundamental concept of forex options is similar to other financial markets, there is a slightly different way in how they are traded. For example, if you buy a USD/EUR options contract, you hold a call option for USD and a put option for EUR.

## Understanding Swaps

Swaps are derivatives that are an agreement between two entities to trade a currency pair in two different instances. Swaps are usually hard to trade for retail investors as it is difficult for them to find an entity that can make a contract with them. Swaps are high valued contracts in the forex market and are used by only large players such as corporations and hedge funds.

## Should I Trade Derivatives?

It is a hard question to answer because even though derivatives are a significant part of the market volume in the forex market, they are extremely risky and are often not recommended for beginners. If you are interested in derivatives, we suggest you take separate training about them for better results.

# Different Trading Strategies in the Forex Market

To get familiar with different trading methods in a forex market, using a demo account instead of a real account is recommended. Understanding different trading strategies can be quite overwhelming, especially if you are starting with forex trading. Irrespective of the trading method you prefer to use, remember that combining the basic forex trading mechanism, technical, and fundamental analysis is important for better results.

Note: No particular strategy is perfect for everyone. Every trading strategy has advantages, disadvantages, and characteristics.

## Understanding Position Trading

A position trader ignores short-time price fluctuations and decides to hold a position for a long time after a thorough fundamental analysis and longer-term technical analysis. Unfortunately, position trading works only with a set of popular currencies and is extremely difficult to estimate whether or not an unpopular currency can sustain well in the long term. This uncertainty forces position traders to be extremely patient and wait longer to have higher returns on their investment.

Usually, fundamental analysis is used to determine the longer-term potential of a particular currency, whereas technical analysis predicts short-term changes in currency prices. As a position trader, you need to make sure that your technical analysis focuses on long-term price fluctuations. Having a sound knowledge of technical analysis can help you to determine entry time and exit strategies.

Important skills for a position trader:

1. A good grip on political and economic news is important as the currency's value can decrease or increase with consistent bad and good reforms by the government.
2. Forex traders need to be closely following megatrends that are changing the world. These megatrends can help a trader predict future price movements. For example, artificial intelligence technology is a megatrend.
3. Black swan events such as natural calamities, pandemics, and terrorist attacks cannot affect position traders as they do for day traders.

### *Understanding Swing Trading*

Swing trading is one of the popular trading methods in a forex market. The important characteristic of the forex market is that it consists of both large and small fluctuations. A swing trader aims to find these swings (price movements) in the market and take advantage of them to see an entry and exit point.

Unlike position traders, swing traders hold their positions for considerably less time. Position traders usually hold their positions for more than a few months, whereas swing traders usually exit their trades within a few days or, during some exceptions, it may take some weeks. For a swing trader, it is important to understand price oscillations in the market for a currency. Prices can usually move to and fro again and again. Traders can observe these inflection points only with advanced technical analysis mastery.

Important Skills for a Swing Trader:

1. Knowing and applying concepts such as reversal patterns, trend lines, moving averages, and support/resistance levels can help a swing trader, especially when the market is volatile.

2. As a swing trader, you need to be aware of stop losses to minimize risks and not lose your profits.

3. Knowledge of fundamental analysis is required for predicting prices. However, analysis of different political and economic factors may not be necessary for a swing trader.

### *Understanding Day Trading*

An intraday trader enters and exits their position within a trading day. The popularity of day trading in the foreign exchange market is because of the huge price fluctuations in the market. Intraday traders exploit this sensitivity to price changes and gain profits within less time.

Intraday traders have very little time to conduct fundamental analysis on the currency they were betting upon due to limited time. Moreover, the market changes rapidly, and so Intraday traders entirely depend on technical indicators to estimate the market's direction.

### **What Will Intraday Traders Do?**

Intraday traders need to understand dependence indicators such as moving averages, oscillating indicators, and relative strength indicators in charts to estimate the currency price movement.

Intraday traders should also focus on support and resistance levels. In an extremely volatile market, the prices will often fluctuate between the support and resistance lines due to bullish and bearish investors trying to trade in their way.

### *Understanding Reverse Trading*

Reverse trading is a trading strategy where traders actively follow the news outlets and proceed with the public's exact opposite sentiment. Reverse traders believe that media outlets publish information and make general people aware of an investment opportunity. Hearing this news, retail investors will flood the market and will increase the price. However, this sudden surge in price will cause capital not to push up further or reflect a bearish trend by big players such as hedge funds and private banks.

For example, when the EUR was strong and had a significant impact on the world economy, people started to bet on it. However, after ten years, EUR did not give strong profits to the investors.

**What Will Reverse Traders Do?**

Analyze the news, public sentiment towards the currency and will bet oppositely. Then, they will either sell their positions or will short them.

*Understanding News Traders*

Unlike reverse traders, news traders entirely depend on the news from media outlets to pick their winners in the trade. News traders will patiently wait for information regarding reports, economic reforms, or trade rules. Then, they will analyze them as quickly as possible to decide their winners for both position and day trading.

How to be an effective news trader:

1. Follow all the government organization websites and their reports.
2. Only believe the verified information. Please check the authenticity of the authors of a trending blog or social media post.
3. Follow influencers in social media to easily access the important news related to the market or your currency.

*Understanding Carry Trading*

Carry trading is one of the simplest and most popular trading strategies due to its high return factor. A trader needs to buy a currency with a high yield or interest rate against the currency with a low-interest currency in carry trading. When you buy the currency with high-interest currency, the brokerage will pay you the interest difference.

For example, let us suppose that the interest rate of CHF is 6% and the USD is 3%. Then, when you go long on the CHF/USD pair, you participate in a carry trade strategy. Therefore, the broker will pay you the difference between the interest rates of 3% to your account.

## Why is Carry Trade Better?

Carry trading helps you to use your leverage effectively. Also, remember that you will be paid interest for your whole leveraged amount but not the margin amount. This makes it extremely profitable in returns.

## Risks in Carry Trading

The currency pairs that support carry trading are generally very volatile. This makes you extremely alert when following this strategy, as a small turn of events can drain your whole amount within no time.

Ensure that you follow efficient risk management strategies to counter back volatility and liquidity problems in a forex market.

## *Understanding Trend Trading*

Trend traders firmly believe that markets can be predicted using technical indicators. Therefore, estimating the future by following the historical price movements is a primary skill for trend traders.

Trend traders usually prefer to go long-term with their positions because trends happen over a long time, unlike short-term movements, which are good for scalpers.

## What are Trends?

Trends are technical analysis indicators that forex traders can use to predict the market change over time. Trends are usually repeated and can help trend traders find a perfect position for entering and exit strategies.

There are three types of trends:

1. **Uptrend:** In an uptrend, the market price of the currency pair increases in value. So when you observe the patterns and find higher highs and higher lows in the charts, then that currency pair is experiencing an uptrend.
2. **Downtrend:** In a downtrend, the market price of the currency pair decreases in value. So when you observe patterns and find lower lows and lower highs, then that currency pair goes through a downtrend.
3. **Sidetrends:** When you analyze the price charts and find nothing but short price fluctuations, it is called a side trend. However, trend traders usually don't care about side trends.

Trend trading is popular and is less risky when compared to other trading strategies in the forex market. In the coming chapters of this book, we will discuss different technical analysis topics such as moving averages, RSI trend indicators for trend trading effectively.

# Chapter 3: Currency Pairs And Outlook

The fact that currencies in the platform are traded in pairs is confusing for beginners. Forex traders need to be aware that instead of investing in a single currency like stocks, in the forex market you will decide a currency's future by comparing it with another currency. There are two types of currency pairs and as a forex investor, knowing about them is necessary.

## What Are The Types of Currency Pairs?

Generally, currency pairs can be divided into two types by the level of importance:

1. Major currency pairs
2. Cross currency pairs

*Major Currency Pairs*

These are the currency pairs that are most liquid and which involve USD in the pair. As most forex traders trade by judging the performance of USD, the majors have a highly volatile nature. Therefore, major currency can be further divided into majors and commodity pairs.

Here are the majors:

- EUR/USD—Here EUR stands for Euro and USD stands for United States Dollar
- GBP/USD—Here GBP stands for British Pound and USD stands for United States Dollar
- USD/CHF—Here USD stands for United States Dollar and CHF stands for Swiss Franc
- USD/JPY—Here USD stands for United States Dollar and JPY stands for Japanese Yen

The other commodity pairs:

- USD/CAD

- NZD/USD
- AUD/USD

Whenever we discuss forex trading, we are usually talking about major currency pairs. These pairs are trendy and react to any news that the U.S. is involved in.

### *Cross Currency Pairs*

The U.S. dollar, known as the vehicle currency, has been used as a reserve currency for many years. As a result, almost 80% of the forex transactions have USD involved in it. However, with the introduction of currency crosses, we can now directly convert any currency to another without dealing with USD.

Some popular examples of cross currencies are GBP/EUR, GBP/JPY, and CHF/EUR.

**Why Do Forex Investors Need to be Aware of Currency Crosses?**
The U.S. dollar, being the world's reserve currency, is used for the transaction of oil and other commodities. This is the reason why many countries keep U.S. dollars in their central banks. For example, it is believed that China alone has 3 trillion USD in its reserves.

This necessity of USD in international commodity transactions makes it an important factor for speculators. All the time in the forex market, speculators will be betting about the prospect of USD. This speculation makes the USD volatile for some of the investors.

Almost all major currency pairs involve USD, and any news related to the U.S. economy will make an impact on them. In addition, the over-dependency on USD speculation has made some of the investor's lookout for opportunities in currency crosses.

Currency crosses will provide you some opportunities when other investors are busy taking a stance about pro-USD or anti-USD. However, unlike majors, currency crosses are also ineffective about the news related to the U.S. economy or politics. This makes cross-currency traders effectively spot the trends that major currency traders cannot.

Another reason why many traders are interested in cross-currency pairs is that they offer high interest rates. You usually receive interest when you sell a currency. Major currencies have lower interest rates, whereas currency crosses offer high-interest rate differentials.

**What to Remember Before Trading Cross Currencies:**

1. Cross currency pairs have less liquidity, and sometimes large institutions use synthetic cross currency pairs to trade in high volume. Even retail traders can create synthetic (or interlinking) cross currency pairs to escape from the problems of low liquidity.
2. Only yen and euro crosses are popular with forex traders, and any other cross currency is referred to as obscure cross-currency as they have very few spikes and offer fewer profits for all the parties involved.
3. Some brokers may restrict the leverage options or provide only 20:1 leverage options if you trade only in cross currency pairs.

**How to Use Cross Currencies to Trade Majors**

Many forex traders cannot risk their portfolios by including cross currency pairs which are volatile and unpredictable because of fewer fundamentals. So, they use these cross-currency price charts to understand the movement and momentum of the market.

For example, if a trader wants to invest in USD/JPY, he will verify his decision by checking the relative strength of JPY with other currencies such as CHF or CAD.

# Major Currencies Outlook

As a forex trader, you need to have a good grip on the economies of the major currency pairs. Understanding the underlying economies of these majors can help you to make smart decisions while doing forex trading. USD, EUR, GBP, CHF, CAD, AUD, NZD, and JPY are known as the major currencies.

### *United States Dollar (USD)*

The USD is the most important of all the currencies that are traded in the forex market. The United States of America is a world superpower and has the largest economy in the world. It has the highest gross domestic product (or GDP) of any other country globally and is home to multinational companies such as Apple, Google, Tesla, and Microsoft. The U.S. is fundamentally a service-based company and controls most of the Information Technology Sector. However the U.S. also depends on infrastructure, health, and manufacturing industries.

The U.S. also holds more foreign savings than any other country. Almost 35% of the foreign reserves that exist are accounted for by the U.S. This makes the U.S. the base currency for many trades in the forex market. Almost 80% of the forex trades happen by involving USD.

The U.S. also accounts for more exports and imports than any other country. Canada is the country with the largest exports from the U.S. whereas China accounts for most imports to the U.S.

### Importance of Federal Reserve

The Federal Reserve has the ultimate power to declare monetary policies in the U.S. The Federal Reserve is not subjected to any political pressures, and it will make all decisions regarding fiscal and monetary policies. It has a 12 member committee known as the Federal Open Market Committee (or FOMC) and is entirely regulated. Every month the federal reserve releases a report regarding the economic performance of the country.

### Why Should You Care About USD?

Forex traders need to be thorough with all the fundamentals related to USD because it accounts for most trades. In one way or another, the U.S. economy controls world trade and economy. USD is also called a safe-haven currency as many foreign investors use it as a reserve currency.

### Euro (EUR)

The European Economic and Monetary Union (or EMU) is a group of 19 countries that share the Euro as their primary currency. France, Germany, Spain, and Italy are some of the countries that partake in it. EMU accounts for the second-largest economy in the world after the U.S.

Many investors are enthusiastic about investing in EUR because there are great capital flows for the Euro. However, in the initial days, European Union countries could not attract any investments from the foreign reserves. This is because the European Union has been inconsistent due to countries leaving and joining again. This gave a wrong signal to the investors, and many instead considered USD a safe investment because it gives consistent returns to the forex traders.

The major advantage of EUR over USD is that the EUR depends mostly on exports to stabilize the economy. All superpowers such as the U.S., China, and Russia depend on European nations for various exports.

## Importance of European Central Bank

All the European nations that recognize EUR as their currency need to rely on the European Central Bank (ECB) for monetary policies. The ECB is regulated and holds a superior value in the world economy. The ECB's main goal is to stabilize the exchange rate of the Euro.

## Why Should You Care About the EUR?

The EUR is the second most reserved currency and has recently been recommended by forex investors as it has less deficit capital, unlike the U.S. China and Russia also support EUR to counter the U.S. trade market. Over the next few years, where analysts expect a trade war between the superpowers of the world, it is smart to invest in EUR as it is considered more stable and has fewer price fluctuations.

### *British Pound (GBP)*

Great Britain was one of the world's superpowers until World War II. However, after World War II, it did not expand its industrialization ability, and as of 2020, industrialization occupies only a small portion of its GDP. Right now, Britain is a service-oriented economy with an efficient banking system. It is also a trade deficit country, with most of its exports going to the United States and imports coming from Germany.

The problem with GBP is that it is often in the news due to its involvement with the European Union. Brexit has made a significant impact on its exchange rate, and uncertainty about effective monetary policies is also why many investors are moving away from GBP as a trading option.

## Why Should You Consider GBP?

The Bank of England is very well regulated and reports GDP and other potential indexes that can be a good resource for fundamental analysts. It, however, gives a higher interest rate than USD and is thus used in the forex market by speculators. It is also the most liquid currency in the forex market.

### *Swiss Franc (CHF)*

Switzerland, though not even being in the top 10 largest economies in the world, is still the home for efficient banking and financial, monetary systems. It accounts for a large sum of foreign currencies and is the wealthiest country on a per capita basis. Switzerland is also home for a complex insurance system that foreigners support.

Many private investments from the underdeveloped and developing economies reach offshore accounts in Switzerland due to their highly efficient banking system.

Swiss national bank is the most regulated monetary system in the world. All the policies that are introduced to its financial system have a great impact on the economy. Many forex traders consider the Swiss Franc safest because it is a safe-haven currency.

### *Japanese Yen (JPY)*

Forex trading is extremely popular in JPY, and many Asian investors, including Chinese investors, place their trades using offshore accounts in the Japanese currency. Japan is the third-largest economy in the world and is famous for its work culture. Japan is also a home for excellent manufacturing and infrastructure companies. Until 2001, most of the American exports were from Japan. Japanese culture such as anime, manga, and video game consoles are usually intriguing for American demographics.

However, in the past decade, the impact of Chinese advancements has reduced the power of Japan in the world economy. However, JPY still provides great opportunities for those who are interested in investing in it. Japan has one of the strongest banking systems, and it also has a complex monetary policy-making authority to control the economy in a stabilized state. As a result, Japan is considered a direct proxy for Asian investors.

### *Australian Dollar (AUD)*

Australia is the twelfth largest economy globally, but it has a good per capita basis, making it a good investment choice for traders. Australia has a service-based economy and relies mostly on Asian countries such as China and Japan. However, this interdependence on Asian pacific countries for exports has made the exchange rates fall for AUD. Australia is also not doing well in the industrial and manufacturing sector due to a lack of innovative economic policies that can help to set up more industries.

With the exponential growth of China nowadays, we can say that Australia now has a good chance of becoming one of the most popular currencies worldwide. The Reserve Bank of Australia also provides the highest interest rate than any other country, and thus it becomes a good short-term currency option for forex traders who need to receive rollover interest.

The Reserve Bank of Australia controls and decides the monetary policies of AUD. It also takes certain measures to stabilize both the economy and exchange rates of the currency.

Australia has a high correlation with commodity prices, and thus if you are interested in betting your currency pair by observing the prices of commodities, then AUD can be a great choice. AUD is also used extensively by carry traders.

### New Zealand Dollar (NZD)

New Zealand is a very small country, but it has an efficient service and manufacturing company. In recent years the exports from New Zealand have been sent to the European Union, and thus the EUR/NZD currency pair has a good exchange rate and is currently being traded well in the forex market. New Zealand is also well regulated and controls the fiscal risks that both the economy and currency may face. Australia is the leading exporter for New Zealand, and European countries, along with China, imports many products to New Zealand.

The Reserve Bank of New Zealand controls the interest rates and stabilizes the exchange rates related to NZD. Therefore, it has a strong correlation with AUD, making NZD/USD one of the popular counter currencies in the forex market.

### Canadian Dollar (CAD)

Canada is the eleventh largest economy globally and depends mostly on natural resources and the manufacturing sector. Canada mostly depends on its exports because of oil and gold. In the 1990s, the new trade policies also helped Canada have a good relationship with the USA. This free trade agreement helped to strengthen the CAD against the USD.

The Central Bank of Canada decides both fiscal and monetary policies. Therefore, it helps to stabilize the currency and not let it face any inflation. One of the major reasons forex traders consider CAD is that it has a great correlation with USD and higher interest rates.

*Chinese Yuan (CNY)*

The Chinese government has pegged its exchange value to the USA. Therefore, if the USD increases its value, then the Yuan will increase, and if the USD decreases its value, then the Yuan will decrease. Therefore, many have claimed that China is a currency manipulator and that the Yuan is undervalued at this time.

There are rumors that the Chinese government has been thinking about changing their exchange laws but still, there is a long way to go. Many economists also feel that China has an unfair advantage due to pegged currency, thereby making China the second-largest economy in the world.

Despite not being in the forex market, China influences the world forex market. Many countries, including the U.S., are now dependent on Chinese exports, and thus any new laws that target Chinese trade relations can impact the market movement. Australia's economy is entirely dependent on China these days due to the increase in their trade relations.

If you are interested in trading with AUD and EUR, you should watch out for Chinese economic reports and their trade war with the U.S.

## What Next?

By now, you have a good understanding of the forex market and the different major currencies involved in the market. However, to improve trading skills to predict the market movement, you need to understand the importance of fundamental and technical analysis that we will discuss in the next chapters.

# Chapter 4: Fundamental Analysis

Traders usually depend on two philosophies known as fundamental and technical analysis to predict market movements. However, there is much debate between traders in the forex market about a better philosophy to predict market movements effectively. Fundamental analysis is used by position and swing traders to judge the currencies based on different economic reports and data. This chapter will discuss the factors that can help a fundamental analyst find the winners for the trade.

## What is Fundamental Analysis?

In fundamental analysis, traders analyse the currency prices using the economic, social and political aspects. Using these factors, traders analyse the supply and demand that exists in the foreign exchange market. Moreover, using these indicators, they estimate the market momentum over both the short and long term. However, remember that using fundamental analysis as a day trader is extremely impractical because you have very little time to make trade decisions. Therefore, fundamental analysts believe that at least two weeks of effective research is essential for finding better winners in the market.

## How Fundamental Analysis Works

In simple words, fundamental analysts believe that supply and demand decide the value of the price. They also believe that supply and demand depend entirely on the country's political, economic, and social aspects. If there is a limited supply, then the demand and the price of the currency will rise. If there is less demand and more supply, then the currency price will decline.

*What to do as a Fundamental Analyst*

As a fundamental analyst, you need to be aware of different issues in the country of the currency you are betting upon. This section has provided various factors that can help a fundamental analyst judge the currency price movement in both long and short terms. All the factors mentioned below will have a relationship between market supply and demand and will directly impact the forex prices of the currencies.

# The Economic Situation of a Country

The relative economic strength helps a trader to understand the rising or decline exchange rates of the currency.

For example, before World War I and II, Britain was known to have the most industrialised economy and had strong economic strength. However, over time after the war, due to inflation and lack of industrial innovation, the British pound has decreased in value and has been replaced by the U.S. dollar. The U.S., unlike Britain, increased its economic strength after the war and has since been called the base currency and occupies a place in most of the forex trades that happen.

*How to Judge the Economic Situation of a Country*

There are many factors to consider by a fundamental analyst in order to judge the economic situation of a country. We have provided some of them in the below section.

*The Economic Development of a Country*

A country's development is estimated usually based on the increase in a country's exports. When export trade increases, the currency exchange rate is firm, and both fiscal revenue and expenditure will be in a good state.

However, if a country's exports decrease, then the fiscal deficit will increase, and inflation will occur. As a result, inflation will lead to both unemployment and a decrease in per capita.

Based on the estimated export figures, we usually divide countries into developed, developing, and under-developed categories.

**What Does Economic Development Mean?**

When there is economic development, there will be an increase in income for every individual. The country will start to produce more industries and infrastructure to meet its demand for exports. The overall happiness index of individuals will also increase along with other factors such as labour productivity, innovation in domestic products and lower-cost production.

As a fundamental analyst, a forex trader needs to analyse all these reports mentioned above should analyse whether a country's economy is developing or staying firm or decreasing. Usage of reports, indexes, and news articles can help you get a good idea about the country's development.

1. **Understanding Balance of Payments:** Every country has international debt to clear, and if this balance increases, it will then affect the exchange rates in the forex market. Every year during the budget sessions, countries will release their international debut for the investors. Ensure that there is a decrease in the debt so that the interests paid by the governments will decrease, which directly increases the economy.

2. **Inflation:** Inflation is a complex concept to understand, even for economists. It roughly means that when the governments increase the circulation of the paper currencies more than the demand, then their value will decrease and make the price of commodities increase.

The problem of higher inflation has recently been observed in both Zimbabwe and Venezuela. When inflation rates increase, the exchange rates will increase, weakening both exports and the economic system. In addition, higher inflation rates will also lead to unemployment, crime and a decrease in the happiness index of the citizens.

**What to Do when Faced with Inflation**

As a fundamental analyst, you need to be carefully following the inflation rates of a currency. This is because both higher and lower inflation can be a problem for the economy. So analyse inflation rates from private agencies to be more accurate about your prediction.

*Impact of Government on Currency Prices*

In a centralised economy, the government controls the flow of the currency and they use institutions such as central banks to regulate the rules of the currency flow. The government's intervention and its policies on the flow of currency can also result in the change of the exchange rates.

Some factors that may affect the exchange rates of a currency in the forex market are mentioned below.

## Fiscal Policy and Monetary Policy

Countries announce fiscal and monetary policies to support both local businesses and multinational companies in a country. When an economy is declining, these policies can impact the economy from a long term perspective.

All these policies will increase the country's macroeconomic situation and help the currency strengthen its values in the foreign exchange market. However, in the short term, when the fiscal and monetary policies are announced, there will be a change in interest rates and a lot of capital inflow occurs, thus decreasing the value of the currency for some time.

### What to Do

As a fundamental analyst, you need to closely follow all the fiscal and monetary policies that a government has announced.

Understand from both a logical and practical way how these policies can impact the government.

1. Are the policies good?
2. How will these policies help to increase local businesses and exports?
3. What are the disadvantages of these policies?
4. Will these policies impact the economy of the country in a good or bad way?
5. Are there any historical examples related to these policies? How did the economy evolve after these reforms?

### Control of Central Bank

Governments authorise central banks to do any measures to make the currency be stabilised. For example, if the currency value increases in the foreign exchange market, then the central banks are authorised to liquidate their international reserves to their local currency. Similarly, when the value of currency decreases, the central bank will buy some foreign reserves to stabilise the currency value.

Central banks hold a superior value in the foreign exchange market. Their main goal is to make the currency stabilised, and sometimes few central banks take desperate measures to control the exchange rates of their currency.

**What to Do**
Ensure that you carefully follow how the central bank of your preferred currency is reacting to the currency's performance in the foreign exchange market. Fundamental analysts also analyse the central bank reports to find a pattern relating to their functioning.

# How to Analyse Economic Data as a Fundamental Analyst

Data is everywhere. All fundamental analysts love to analyse data to find patterns and develop their predictions for the market prices. Nowadays, hedge funds and other big market players use high-level computers to analyse data and predict the winners. Over the next decade, both data analysis and machine learning software will improve their abilities to predict the winners.

No matter how much software you use, a forex trader needs to be aware of the important economic data he needs to collect. In this section, we provide some of the reports that you need to be constantly analysing to predict the market moves of a currency or a currency pair.

### *What is Economic Data?*

Both governments and private agencies provide economic data to judge the performance of the different sectors of the economy. Nowadays, due to rapid digitalisation, most reports are digital footprints and can be easily traced. However, there is still a problem with publishing manipulated data in underdeveloped countries. To counter them, it is better to use private agency reports if you are trading counter currencies.

Economic data is also most useful for long-term traders because they focus mainly on macroeconomic situations. However, if you are a short term trader, you need to be aware of microeconomic indicators, which are mostly hard to track.

## Gross Domestic Product (GDP)

GDP is usually used to define the total value of all the final products and services that the country has produced on a quarterly or yearly basis. Thus, GDP is usually used to estimate the economic performance of a country.

If there is an increase in the overall GDP compared to the previous year, then it can be understood that the economy is booming. On the contrary, if there is a decrease in the GDP compared to the previous year, it can be understood that the economy is declining. By comparing the GDP of the countries, economists usually predict the exchange rates of the currencies. GDP can also be used to express both the expansion and recession in the economy.

Some countries also declare nominal GDP without mentioning the inflation rates that highly affect the economy. As a fundamental analyst, you need to be aware of GDP and nominal GDP to predict the exchange rates in the forex market.

### Who Will Publish GDP Reports?

Every government releases its GDP reports using different firms and departments. For example, in the United States, the department of commerce is responsible for analysing and publishing GDP reports. Every country uses its strategies and factors to measure the GDP rate. You can also depend on private agencies sometimes to have more accurate information.

### Purchasing Managers Index (PMI)

Indexes are used to estimate the performance of a particular sector or management based on their research and data. For example, every month the Institute for Supply Management (ISM) releases a document about purchasing managers index.

This index provides valuable information about the performance of the top eight industries which play a key role in the U.S. economy. Most of the fundamental analysts use this report to estimate the economic growth in the U.S.

### What to Know

When there is a steep 50% increase in the PMI index, it can be a good indicator for growth in the manufacturing economy. On the other hand, a 50% decrease in the PMI index can trigger a decrease in the manufacturing economy. Therefore, small changes can be considered as a signal for a stable economy in the manufacturing sector.

As a forex trader, you need to carefully follow the PMI index because many experienced forex traders believe that it is the most accurate and gives a clear view about where the economy is headed.

## Durable Goods Orders

Durable goods are items which have a life of more than three years. For example, military equipment and high-level automobiles such as planes and ships fall under this category.

When there is an increase in the production of these durable goods, it can be said that there is a surge in the economy. Every month, the U.S. Department of Commerce releases information about durable good orders for investors and researchers.

## Equipment Utilisation Rate

Every country has infrastructure and equipment to create both export and domestic products. Therefore, it is important to analyse how much equipment is being utilized by the manufacturers.

Every month the United States' Federal Reserve Board publishes the Industrial Production and Capacity Utilization. If there is a utilisation rate of 95%, then the economy is performing well. On the other hand, if the equipment utilisation rate is below 90%, then it can be observed that the economy is in a declining state.

These factors will impact the foreign exchange rate because they directly impact the export numbers in impacting industries such as automobiles, heavy metals, durable, non-durable, and public utilities.

## Employment and Unemployment Rates

It is hard to track unemployment data because governments usually ignore tracking these rates as effectively as others. Usually, an increase in 5% of the unemployment rates can be termed a disaster from an economic perspective.

Both inflation and employment rates are usually interlinked. Rescissions also do have a high impact on unemployment rates. Sometimes international factors can also result in losing jobs, especially for the IT sector, which is now a major chunk of the economy.

### What to Do

As a fundamental analyst, you need to track unemployment rates for the most popular sectors in the economy. However, tracking non-agricultural economies can be a tough task, and thus the usage of private agency reports is recommended for better predictions.

## Leading Index

This is a particular index that predicts the economy's improvement over six to nine months based on various statistical processing factors. The leading index mechanism includes the analysis of 11 financial and non-financial sectors to predict its index.

It uses some or all of the following to predict the economy:

- Investment opportunities and rates

- Market demand changes

- Number of orders

- All the enterprise information

- Other psychological indicators such as politics

**Retail Sales**

Every business makes sales and usually depends entirely on these prices and profits to increase their production and make challenging decisions that can impact their growth.

Retail and wholesale sales both are important for the development of the economy. As a fundamental analyst, you need to make sure the retail sales are performing on par with the exports in the country.

Every quarter, the United States government and public traded companies will release their retail sales to encourage long-term and short-term investors to participate in the trend.

**Consumer Price Index (CPI)**

When there is inflation or recession, the consumers will start to reduce their product consumption. For example, a decline in automobile sector sales means that the consumers are not interested in spending money due to recession or bad economy.

The consumer price index is used to estimate this factor using various statistical methodologies. First, governments make sure that the CPI is not increasing consistently, and if it does, governments introduce new regulators to make the CPI decrease. In addition, many governments decrease the taxation rates on sectors that are performing badly.

The consumer price index also directly affects the forex exchange rates because when CPI increases, the economy worsens and thus, the value of the currency will decrease compared to other international currencies. The U.S. Bureau of Labor Statistics publishes data every month regarding CPI.

**Producer Price Index (PPI)**

Countries rely on farmers, manufacturers, and small businesses to increase the producer price index. Therefore, PPI is an important indicator for economic growth, and an increase in PPI means a significant decrease in the inflation rates.

It is always better for a country if there is rampant production in the commercial sector by the producers. This is because small businesses are the backbone of a country's economy. The U.S. Bureau of Labor Statistics releases the PPI reports every month.

## Industrial Production Report

Industries are used for the production of both raw materials and innovative products. Therefore, as a fundamental analyst, you need to have a detailed report about all the industries and their production details for judging their future movements in the market.

An increase in industrial production consistently means that the economy is booming, which is a good factor for strengthening the currency in the foreign exchange market.

## Employment Cost Index

While the employment and unemployment reports discussed before only provide information based on the whole sectors, the employment cost index provides information based on different sectors.

As a fundamental analyst, you need to point out the sectors that have a decrease in the index and should find out the reasons for the decrease in wages. For example, fewer wages in non-agricultural industries can lead to a decrease in the happiness index.

## Housing Operation Rate/Existing Home Sales Rate

The housing industry is the most important in the US economy. We all know about the U.S. housing bubble crisis that occurred in 2008 and how it had caused recession worldwide. As a fundamental analyst, you need to analyse the increase in private and group houses in the market.

Group houses are more controversial to analyse because they may not be sold after the construction, and this may lead to losses for both the owner and the economy. On the other hand, private houses are considered a good sign for the economy as the number of workers in the construction company will increase.

The U.S. Department of Housing & Urban Development produces the data regarding home sales every month, and analysing it can help you estimate its impact on the currency transaction value in the forex market.

## Trade Balance

Usually a country requires both exports and imports to continue the economy. Therefore, a lack of exports can impact the economy and cause a trade deficit, whereas if exports are greater than the imports, it is called a trade surplus.

The trade balance is a situation where exports will be equal to imports. The problem with a trade deficit is that it will directly impact the exchange trade of the currencies. Therefore, all countries try to achieve a trade balance to make their exchange rates stay stabilized.

The United States Department of Commerce publishes a trade balance report every month to explain the total export and import figures. As a fundamental analyst, you need to observe these statistics while trading the major currency pairs carefully.

## Personal Income and Expenditure

The Bureau of Economic Analysis (BEA) publishes every month a report about average personal income and expenditure. This report provides information about the end consumer in the country and how they are spending their money on every sector.

The report also provides information about different demographics such as age, state, and gender. In addition, it has two indexes known as personal income index and personal consumption index.

Fundamental analysts can use the personal income index to predict future consumption and its impact on the exchange rate of currency, whereas the consumption expenditure index can determine inflation and its impact on the exchange rate in the forex market.

## Interest Rate

Interest rates are the important macroeconomic factors a fundamental analyst needs to focus on for predicting the prices of the currencies. Central banks or the monetary associations that control the currency decide the interest rates depending on factors such as liquidity, foreign reserves, and inflation.

When the economy is booming, the interest rates will be lowered, and if the economy is in distress, then the interest rates will increase, making it difficult for forex traders to hold the positions.

Fundamental analysts also should focus on rate parity which is used to balance the foreign exchange market.

Usually, the U.S. provides lower interest rates due to holding a lot of foreign reserves. Many forex traders use secondary majors such as GBP or AUD to effectively manage their trades if there is an increase in interest rates. The USD provides lower interest rates because of the U.S. treasury bills and bonds market.

The U.S. federal open market decides the open interest rates of the USD and thus should be carefully followed by forex traders to decide the counter currencies they need to invest effectively.

**Current Account**

A current account is known as the current balance of payments a country at the moment holds. If it is positive, then the current account is called to be in the surplus state, and if it is in the negative, it is called to be in a deficit state.

What is included in the current account?

1.  All the commodities that are either imported or exported will be included in the current account.
2.  All the services, charges, taxation bills, port charges will also be included in the current account.
3.  Current account will also focus on investment income that comes to individuals in the form of dividends, savings, mutual funds and various other investments.
4.  All the donations to non-profit organizations or relief coming from any foreign institutions will also be included.

The U.S. Department of Commerce every two and half months will produce the reports for the current account. Therefore, as a fundamental analyst, you should thoroughly revise the current account statistics before trading a currency pair.

**Budget Deficit**

Every government has a budget every year, and they need to introduce certain reforms for every sector. However, sometimes if their expenses fall way above the budget that a country can afford, it is called the budget deficit.

Having a budget deficit is not good for the economy, and it will have a significant impact on the exchange rates in the forex market. Therefore, the Ministry of Finance in India usually publishes if there is any deficit budget.

# How to Analyze Market Factors

Fundamental analysts should also consider various market factors before starting a trade. For example, sometimes price fluctuations will happen entirely due to speculation and big player's manipulation in the market.

## Speculation

Forex trading is often a tit-for-tat game between the monetary institutions such as central banks and international speculative players such as hedge funds, multinational companies, and international private banks.

There is always a winner in the game, and it should be understood that government institutions use it to strengthen the value of their currency, whereas speculative players do it to gain profits.

Understanding speculation and finding out speculative trends during the trade is essential for having a good entry and exit point.

## Market Risk Appetite

Market risk appetite mentions how much an individual retail trader in the market is willing to risk when you trade. However, this is just an estimation, and it is just used to represent the overall sentiment of the retail traders in the market.

If traders are ready to risk, then there is a chance that they are waiting for an uptrend to happen soon. When there is a risk, there is a reward. Therefore, it is important to understand as a forex trader about market risk appetite before executing your trade.

## Market Forecast

There are many players in the market, and each has their viewpoints about different issues. Therefore, sometimes the total market has different opinions, and they could not correctly estimate future events.

For example, the forex market did not estimate the fall of GBP and the rise of EUR. However, now the GBP has lost its glory, whereas the EUR is the second largest currency in terms of market cap in the forex market.

Market forecast works great for many occasions, but do not follow it just because everyone is doing it. Small profits can be great, but losses can be frustrating.

# Understanding Psychological Factors

Apart from the economic reports mentioned above, fundamental analysts should also care about psychological factors that affect both the market and the traders involved. For example, forex traders can drive the currency exchange prices without any significant change in the economy.

This is because traders sometimes make decisions based on greed and fear. Any news related to interest rates or monetary policies can trigger price changes. However, they may not be implemented or were crossed out considering as rumors in the long run. However, if you are a scalper, then these psychological factors can help you to earn good profits in the long run.

## *Political Events*

Politics and the economy are interlinked. As a fundamental analyst, you need to be carefully following the country's political situations. A rift in the government leaders can cause a decrease in the exchange rate of the currency.

You need to be also closely following international politics to understand the changes in the market. Important international political events can trigger currency prices. Some of these events could be a rise in oil prices due to new Saudi Arabian rules, a trade war between the U.S. and China, or a civil war in Yemen.

## *Black Swan Events*

The market is also very volatile to sudden events known as black swan events, where an event happens that surpasses any planning or foreknowledge. Terrorist attacks, natural calamities, and pandemics can be called black swan events, and they will result in a crash of the whole market. Following emergency news channels is essential for immediately knowing the news and closing your positions as soon as possible.

## *Hot Spot Effect*

In the world of the internet and social media, a small video or tweet can trigger the markets. For example, recently, Elon Musk collapsed the cryptocurrency markets with a single tweet. While the forex market is not as volatile as cryptocurrency markets, it still has the effects of hotspots.

Ensure that you follow all the trending news articles or other media that can help you decide whether or not an exchange rate can be impacted. In addition, transcripts of foreign executives and ministers need to be analyzed before making your trade decisions.

Fundamental analysis often works well for the trader because it analyses most of the factors that change exchange rates. Fundamental analysis, however, is mostly used by position traders and swing traders only due to time constraints. A day trader or scalper will not have sufficient time to verify all this information, and thus, they use a more straightforward trading philosophy known as technical analysis to predict the market movement.

# Chapter 5: Technical Analysis

While fundamental analysis predicts the market based on research, reports and statistical data, the other important philosophy in the forex market deals with charts, technical indicators and the importance of supply and demand. Technical analysis is commonly used by day traders, trend traders and scalpers. Understanding different technical charts may seem like a daunting task initially, but once you start to fall in love with charts, indicators, and trend lines, there is no looking back. This chapter will focus on some of the important technical charts and indicators that forex traders need to know.

## What is Technical Analysis?

In technical analysis, the traders use certain mathematical, logical, and statistical methods to find outlaws that can impact future price changes. Analyzing much historical data and finding similar patterns to enter and exit the trades is also an essential technical analyst skill.

Technical analysis is first used by stock investors to judge the market movement during high trading days. Many day traders soon started to understand the usage of technical indicators and started to implement these analysis tools in everyday trade. Technical analysis is mostly preferred for day traders because macroeconomic factors have less impact on short-term price fluctuations.

*Why Do Traders Use Technical Analysis?*

1. To find an entry point so that they can buy in advance and take profits when the trend goes up.
2. To find an exit point so that they can sell in advance and stop losses when the trend goes down.

As a technical analyst, you need good trading tools and software to look at the historical data based on various parameters. Understanding different kinds of charts is essential for mastering the art of technical analysis.

# Different Types of Charts

There are tons of different types of charts that traders use all around the world. It is important to be consistent while working with charts. However, using many of them may become overwhelming and distracting over time.

## *Line Charts*

These are the most basic graphs that are available for technical analysts. Line charts are also known as dot graphs or star graphs. They are straightforward and simple to understand.

In a line chart, all the closing prices for a trading day will be mentioned in the graph. All these will be connected by a dotted line to easily represent whether there is an uptrend or downtrend in the currency's price. Some traders also represent line charts to represent moving averages instead of closing prices.

Line charts are only used to have a quick grasp of the historical performance of the currency. Therefore, short-term traders such as day traders or scalpers do not rely on line charts as they provide very little information.

## *Histogram*

A histogram is also known as a bar chart and is extremely popular with technical analysts. Unlike the line graph, it provides much detailed information about forex prices.

It will represent the opening and closing prices of a forex currency pair and the day high and low using vertical and horizontal lines. Thus, the bar chart can represent currency prices for a day or a certain period.

### What Does Each Line Represent?
*Bottom vertical line:* Determines the lowest price of the currency pair in the period or for a trading day.

*Top vertical line:* Determines the highest price of the currency pair in the period or for a trading day.

*Horizontal lines:* These bars represent the opening and closing prices for a period or a trading day

As the volatility of the currency pair increases, you will start to see more vertical lines. These charts are also known as OHLC charts as they represent open, high, low and close of a currency pair.

### *Candlestick Charts*

Candlestick charts are similar to bar charts but are more visual and are gripping for technical analysts. The difference between bar charts and candlestick charts is that they are visually more gripping and can easily represent both bearish and bullish trends for a technical analyst.

### How are charts represented?

*Vertical lines:* Just like bar charts, the top and bottom of vertical lines represent the high and close of a currency pair for a particular period. These high/low ranges are also known as shadows.

*Body:* The larger block that is present in the middle is used to represent the difference between the open and close prices. This body is usually represented in different colors for easily finding out bear and bull trends.

### What Colors Are Used?

Usually, if the closing price is more than the open price, bull trends will be represented using white color. Some technical analysts use green for better visual appreciation. Bear trends, on the other hand, are represented using black color. Some other technical analysts use red for better visual appreciation.

### Why are Candlestick Charts Extensively Used?

1. They are great and as they are usually engaging, finding trend patterns is easy compared to bar charts.
2. Much research has gone into candlestick charts, and there are hundreds of patterns that technical analysts can use to identify different conditions in the market.

3. Candlestick charts are very useful while recognizing hidden market movements such as trend reversals and divergence.

**Understanding Candlesticks Anatomy**

While it may seem simple, a lot can be understood with candlesticks. The body in the charts is used to represent the buying or selling of the currency pairs.

For example, if the charts have a longer body, it represents that much action is going in the market to buy or sell currencies. On the other hand, if the charts have a short body, it represents that both bulls and bears are not risking entering into the trade.

- Long white—Bulls pressure
- Short white—Fewer bulls pressure
- Long black—Bears pressure
- Short black—Fewer bears pressure

The shadows that represent both high and low can also be intriguing. For example, if there are long shadows, the action took place far away from open and close prices. On the other hand, if there are long lower shadows, it means the action took place near to the open and close of the currency pair.

# Candlestick Chart Patterns

Knowing some Japanese candlestick chart patterns is essential for the success of a forex trader.

*Spinning Tops*

Spinning tops are one of the popular candlestick chart patterns which represent long lower and upper shadows. In spinning tops, the body is usually very small. Therefore, it can be interpreted as a very little movement between the opening and closing prices which means that both bears and bulls are not ready to decide on the trade.

**How to Use Spinning Tops**

Spinning tops can be used to find reversal patterns in the trade. If during an upward trend you can spot the spinning top, it means that there are no more bulls left, and the price may fall due to this. In the same way, if you find spinning tops during a downward trend, it means that there are no more bears left, and the price may rise due to this.

## *Marubozu*

It is a special candlestick chart pattern without any shadows, but only has a body. It is also famously known as a bald candlestick pattern. We can use marubozu to detect both bullish and bearish reversal patterns.

### White Marubozu

When you find a white marubozu in the chart, the open price is low, and the close price is high. It means that the bulls are taking control of the pattern, and there will likely be an uptrend.

If you find white marubozu during an uptrend, it means that the bullish trend will continue. Conversely, if you find white marubozu during a downtrend, it means that the bearish trend will take a reversal pattern and change to a bullish pattern.

### Black Marubozu

When you find a black marubozu in the chart, the close equals the low, and the open equals the high. Thus, it represents that the bears are taking control of the pattern, and there will likely be a downtrend.

If you find black marubozu during a downtrend, it means that the bearish trend is likely to continue. If you find it during an uptrend, it means that the bullish trend will take a reversal pattern so that the bearish trend starts.

## *Doji*

Doji is one of the popular candlestick chart patterns. It is used along with marubozu to describe the buyer and seller pattern that a technical analyst needs to be aware of. Doji candlestick charts have the same open and close prices. However, they have very little body when represented in the chart.

When you see a doji candlestick chart pattern, it means that both buyers and sellers are confused. There are different types of doji charts. Gravestone doji and dragonfly doji are the ones popular in them.

**What to observe?**

1. If you observe a doji form or many doji forms after a bullish pattern such as white marubozu, it means that the bulls are becoming weak and they do not have the potential to buy more. It means that a bearish trend is going to happen soon.

2. If you observe a doji form or many doji forms after a bearish pattern, such as black marubozu, it means that the bears are weakening, and they do not have the potential to sell more. It means that a bullish trend is inevitable, and an uptrend is going to happen soon.

With a detailed introduction to technical analysis concepts, you are now ready to learn about some of the advanced technical analysis concepts that forex traders should know.

# Understanding Support Line and Resistance Line

Any financial market is a game between bullish and bearish traders. A bullish trader hopes for the price to rise so that the value of his open positions increases. A bearish trader hopes for the price to decrease to sell and buy back the positions at a lower price.

In simple words, bullish traders will increase the exchange rate in forex terminology, whereas bearish traders will decrease the exchange rate.

In this war between bears and bulls, the market prices of a currency usually fluctuate to and fro many times until finally, it either leads to a bullish trend or a bearish trend.

### *What is the Support Line?*

When there is a fluctuation between the prices and the currency's exchange rate starts to decrease, bulls will aggressively start to buy more currency pairs and increase the currency's exchange rate. Usually, this aggressive buying is observed by technical analysts in the chart, and they call it a support line.

*What is the Resistance Line?*

When there is an increase in the currency exchange rates, bears will start to aggressively sell their open position currency pairs to decrease the exchange rates. This is observed by technical analysts using the charts, and they call it the resistance line.

Understand supply and resistance as technical indicators that provide you information about the supply and demand for a currency pair. In the end, if the bullish traders succeed in the war with the bears, there will be a surge in the exchange rate of the currency. On the other hand, if the bearish traders succeed in the war against the bears, there will be a decline in the currency exchange rate.

As a technical analyst, you need to constantly observe the charts to find a support/ resistance line and use them to exit and enter your trades effectively. Nowadays, trading platforms provide this information for all the traders for every open position to manage their trades effectively.

# Understanding Moving Averages

Moving averages are especially used to eliminate the market noise that comes with trade patterns. With the help of moving averages, traders can predict the correct trend direction in the chart. These types of indicators can also be called overlays. The unpredictability in the price directions is usually due to random trades done by retail traders. Using indicators such as moving averages, we can eliminate these irrelevant data and focus on bearish and bullish patterns occurring in the market.

Moving averages are determined using different periods. Usually, there are two types of moving averages known as simple and exponential moving averages.

*How is the Simple Moving Average Calculated?*

To calculate a simple moving average, you need to select a five-period sample for a particular period. For example, let us take 10 minutes as the time frame of the period.

All you need to do is add the closing prices of all the last five 10 minute periods and divide them by five. This will give you a simple moving average.

However, the problem with simple moving averages is that they give bad signals when there is a sudden change in the prices. This is the reason why exponential moving averages are developed.

### *How are Exponential Moving Averages Calculated?*

While using exponential averages, you will give more preference to the recent trades. For example, in a five-period trade, the last three will be given more preference so that the prices with spikes can be correctly represented in the chart.

### *How Does Moving Averages Determine Trends?*

To determine trends, all you have to do is draw the moving averages in the chart and compare them with the real-time price changes. If you observe that the real price changes are above the moving averages, the trend is an uptrend. Conversely, if you find that the real price changes are below the moving averages, the price is a downtrend.

However, you cannot entirely depend on one moving average to make correct predictions. Therefore, ensure that you at least have three moving average indicators to predict the momentum of the prices of the forex currency pairs.

This section will explain some popular technical indicators to help a forex trader for various use cases.

# Bollinger Bands

Technical analysts especially use Bollinger Bands to determine the high volatile situations where the traders have either overbought or oversold the currency pairs.

These upper and lower bands are used to estimate the direction of the volatility. Many traders use the upper band, lower band and middle band to know how spread out the trading is.

Technical analysts can also use advanced Bollinger Indicators such as Bollinger Bounce and Bollinger squeeze to estimate whether an uptrend or downtrend will happen. Finally, the bands use standard deviation and simple moving averages to predict the trends.

# Keltner Channels

Keltner channels are also a technical indicator used to estimate the volatility and predict the price changes for the forex. It is similar to Bollinger Bands, but uses exponential moving averages and Average True range instead of simple moving average and standard deviation. Traders use it especially when there is a flat pattern in the charts.

# Moving Average Convergence Divergence Indicator

A MACD indicator can use moving averages in a complex way to estimate the price changes. In addition, MACD can predict whether a trend is going to take a bullish or bearish turn. Determining this is very important for a day trader, especially at the end of the trading day.

### *What Can We Do With a MACD?*

MACD usually uses three numbers to represent its findings:

1. The first number represents the number of periods where the momentum of moving averages is faster.
2. The second number represents the number of periods where the momentum of moving averages is slower.
3. The third number represents the difference between the first and second periods mentioned above.

For example, if the number is 15, 54, 39. It precisely says that 15 bars have a faster-moving average, 54 bars have a slower moving average, and 39 is the difference between these two moving averages.

*How to Trade Using MACD*

Before trading, you need to know about signal indicators. A signal indicator is formed by the moving averages of the MACD indicator.

Now, to understand trends, we need to map both MACD and signal. As MACD is a faster-moving average and signal is a slower moving average, if we can find a crossover, the trend pattern will change soon. We can use a histogram to find the distance between these indicators and decide whether an uptrend or downtrend will happen.

# Parabolic SAR

A Forex Trader needs to know how to find stop and reversal trends that can help you to know when to exit the trade. SAR is an abbreviation for Stop and Reversal.

Parabolic SAR is represented using dots, and it has a simple way to determine when to exit the trend. All you have to do is whether the dots are above the candlestick patterns or below the candlestick patterns.

1. If the dots are above the candlestick patterns, it means that it is time to sell your forex positions.
2. If the dots are below the candlestick patterns, it means that it is time to buy your forex positions.

This technical indicator, however, cannot help you if the market is sideways.

# Stochastic Indicator

A stochastic indicator is a technical indicator that can also help you determine when a trend is going to end. Stochastic is considered more reliable than Parabolic SAR. The stochastic indicator uses momentum as a sign to determine whether a trend is going to end or not.

George Lane, who developed it in the 1950s, used a scaled measurement of 0-100 to determine the overbought and oversold conditions.

### How to Determine

1. When the stochastic lines are above 80, represented by a red dotted line, the forex pair is overbought, and it may soon fall. A bearish trader will take advantage of this indication and will exit the trade.
2. When the stochastic lines are below 20, represented by a blue line, the forex pair is oversold and may rise soon. A bullish trader will take advantage of this indication and will enter the trade.

However, remember that the stochastic indicators may stay above 80 or below 20 for a long time. So mix it with other technical indicators to determine when to exit or enter the trade.

## Relative Strength Index (RSI)

RSI provides a much better way to analyze both oversold and overbought situations. It is more reliable during a busy market day. Like the stochastic indicator, RSI is also scaled from 0-100. The advantage, however, that RSI provides is that they provide centerline crossovers to predict the rising bullish or bearish trends.

### How can we use RSI to determine various conditions?

1. If the RSI indicators are below 30, it means that the market is in an oversold condition. This means that there is soon going to be a bullish trend.

2. If the RSI indicators are above 70, it means that the market is in an overbought situation. This means that there is soon going to be a bearish trend.
3. If the RSI indicator is just below 50 and is falling to 30, it is a signal for a bearish trend.
4. If the RSI indicator is just above 50 and is rising to 70, it is a signal for a bullish trend.

Remember that there may be fakeouts. So, make sure that you use them with other technical indicators to predict the correct movement of the forex pair.

## Williams Percent Range (Williams %R)

This is similar to a stochastic indicator but in a more sensible way. When you want to know whether there is a bullish or bearish turn, you can use this indicator for more precise predictions.

Willian %R is used most importantly when the traders need to know whether or not the bull or bear run will continue further. So, instead of a 0-100 level scale, the William %R uses a 0 to negative 100 scale.

*How to Determine:*

1. When you find the indicators near -20, then it means that the currency pair is overbought, and a bearish turn will happen.
2. When you find the indicators near -80, then it means that the currency pair is oversold, and a bullish turn will happen.

## Average Directional Index (ADX)

Technical indicators also consist of non-directional indexes that do not necessarily say whether it is bullish or bearish. However, in trading, it is important to know the strength of the direction irrespective of the movement. So when you are looking out to estimate the strength of a trend, ADX can be extremely helpful.

ADX is also an oscillator with a scale of 0-100. If the reading is below 20, then it is said to be a weak trend. On the other hand, if the readings are above 50, we can call it a strong trend.

ADX can be used when there are signs of trend reversals, but you cannot entirely decide whether it is true or not. ADX can be used to estimate the trend strength and thus the trade reversal probability.

With a clear understanding of technical indicators, you are now all ready to learn about the advanced technicals that a forex trader needs to be aware of.

## What Are Lagging and Leading Indicators?

There are usually two types of indicators in technical analysis. One is lagging indicators and the other one is leading indicators.

A leading indicator hints at the trader before an overbought or oversold situation occurs so that the trader can enter or exit the trade quickly. On the other hand, a lagging indicator does not provide the trend information instantly but will inform you after some time.

You might get a doubt about why lagging indicators are even a thing when leading indicators do the work that we need. However, with leading indicators, there is a catch. They are not necessarily always correct. In fact, for more than 40% of the time, you will be encountering fakeouts.

As a forex trader, it is recommended to use lagging indicators for trending markets and leading indicators for sideways markets.

All the technical indicators explained above can be called oscillators. Oscillators deal with data that move back to and fro between two points. As an investor, oscillators will help you track and recognize trends that drive the same bearish and bullish trends repeatedly. Stochastic, RSI and William %R are some of the very popular oscillators with forex traders. Using oscillators, we can determine trend reversals, uptrend, downtrend and trend continuation.

Forex traders should include both lagging (trend confirming) and leading indicators (oscillators) in a technical analyst's toolbox. You are now aware of the technical indicators to help you find out overbought and oversold conditions to create an entry and exit strategy. We will now proceed further to help you understand the importance of chart patterns as a technical analyst.

# Chart Patterns

Chart patterns can help traders determine the big breakouts in the market by observing and deciphering them. In addition, chart patterns will help you to understand reversal and continuation patterns in much more detail.

**What Are the Advantages of Chart Patterns?**
1. They will help you to find entry signals when there is a rising trend
2. They will help you to find an exit point so that you can take away your profits or cut back your losses

We will discuss some of the popular chart patterns that forex traders need to be aware of.

*Double Top*

A double top is usually formed when there is an extended move up in the prices. Usually, in double top patterns, the price will first reach a top level and bounce to a low to return to the top level again.

As a technical analyst, if you observe the price bouncing off to the same level, we can decide that a reversal will occur soon. When you observe a double top, it is time to liquidate your open positions because the buying pressure has decreased, and bulls will not be as aggressive as before. This gives a chance for bears to sell their positions and decrease the price of the asset value.

Forex traders extensively use double tops during an uptrend. This is because forex traders mostly use double tops to save their profits.

## Double Bottom

Double bottom is also a chart indicator that is used to detect reversal patterns. However, unlike double top, this chart indicator is used by forex traders during a downtrend.

If you observe a trend that indicates that price has reached a bottom and raised again only to reach the bottom again, then it is a double bottom. When you observe a double bottom, you can observe that the selling pressure has decreased, and bulls will soon cause the prices to rise.

## Head and Shoulders

Forex traders exclusively use the head and shoulders pattern to observe reversal patterns during an uptrend. In this pattern, at first, a peak is formed (shoulder) followed by a higher peak (head) and immediately another peak (shoulder). It means that the buying pressure has decreased, and a price drop is going to happen.

You can also use inverse head and shoulder patterns to estimate the reversal trends during a downtrend.

## Bearish Rectangle

When the forex pair's price crosses the support level, and if you observe a rectangle pattern in the charts, it means that there is indecision by the sellers as to whether or not to proceed with the market movement.

When you find a rectangle pattern below the support line, it hints to short the positions and wait for the prices to drop.

*Bullish Rectangle*

When the forex pair's price is just above the resistance level and if you find a rectangle pattern, it means that there is indecision by buyers as to whether or not to proceed with the market movement.

When you find a rectangle pattern just above the resistance line, it means a hint to take long with your position and wait for the prices to rise.

*Bearish Pennant*

When a strong downtrend is going on for a short time, many bears in the trend will close their short positions, leading to price consolidation. At this time, you will observe a symmetrical triangle pattern known as the pennant.

If you observe a bearish pennant, you need to place a short order at the bottom of the pennant and a stop-loss order above the pennant. Stop loss above the pennant can help you to avoid fake-outs in the process.

*Bullish Pennant*

When a strong uptrend is going on for a short time, a small portion of bulls will sell their long positions, making the price consolidate at the same level for some time. At this time, a pennant will form, and you can use it as an indicator to not sell your positions as there will be a much larger uptrend ahead.

If you observe a bullish pattern, make sure that you place a long order above the pennant and a stop-loss order below the pennant to not lose out on any profits.

# Chapter 6: Divergence

Forex trading is home to various trading strategies and philosophies often debated, disputed, and owned by traders. Divergence is one of these trading methods that many forex traders use to gain profits.

## What is Divergence?

Usually, forex traders use technical analysis indicators to predict the price changes in the market. However, there is a problem with technical indicators. You can only find them midway while observing, and for this reason, they are called lagging indicators. To counter this problem, the concept of divergences has emerged. Divergences are known as leading indicators and are extensively used by forex traders to estimate the price trends of a currency pair.

### When Can We Observe A Divergence?

To understand divergence, you need first to know different types of technical analysis indicators, such as an oscillator type indicator. Now, if you observe that the oscillator is heading up and the actual prices are heading down, we can say that divergence occurred.

Remember that if both the indicators are deemed to perform in the same direction, then divergence is minimized.

## Types of Divergence

Divergence is usually determined by either a bearish or bullish trend. A bullish trend means that the price value of an asset is increasing, whereas a bearish trend implies that the price value of the asset is decreasing.

Divergences are usually of two types, and they can be further divided into four based on bullish and bearish phenomena.

1. Regular divergence
   a. Regular bearish
   b. Regular bullish
2. Hidden divergence
   a. Hidden bearish
   b. Hidden bullish

# Understanding Regular Divergence

Regular divergence can be used to predict trend reversals. They can be of both bearish and bullish patterns.

### *Regular Bullish Divergence*

We first need to check the oscillator indicator. If the oscillator shows higher lows and the real-time price changes are lower lows, it can be called a regular bullish divergence.

Technical analysts usually observe this pattern during downtrends and decide that the price is going to rise.

### *Regular Bearish Divergence*

If the oscillator is making a lower high and the real-time price changes are higher high, then you are looking at a regular bearish divergence. The technical analyst usually observes this pattern during downtrends.

This divergence predicts that the price will be reversed and drop, making it a bearish pattern in forex currency prices.

### *What is the Purpose of Regular Divergences?*

Using regular divergences, you can predict when tops and bottoms occur. These can also be effective in determining reversal patterns. As a technical analyst, you will end up using divergence in many of your trades as it is easier to determine with a bit of knowledge.

# Understanding Hidden Divergence

Using regular divergences, we have predicted when a trade reversal is going to happen. Using hidden divergences, we can predict whether or not a continuation will occur in the trend.

As a forex trader, knowing about trend continuation is as essential as a trend reversal. Knowing about trend continuation can make you invest in short-term trades. Many scalpers use this divergence strategy to make some quick gains.

### *What is a Hidden Bullish Divergence?*

Hidden bullish divergence occurs mainly when an uptrend is going on. To spot a hidden divergence, you need to first look at the actual price changes. It will usually be a higher low. If there is no bullish trend further, then the oscillator will also show the same higher low. However, if the oscillator shows a lower low, then the uptrend is likely to continue making it a better place for bull traders.

### *What is a Hidden Bearish Divergence?*

A hidden bearish divergence occurs mainly when a downtrend is going on. First, look at the real-time price changes and confirm there are lower highs in the technical charts. If there is no bearish trend further, then the oscillator will also show lower highs. However, if the oscillator shows higher highs, then the downtrend is likely to continue making it a better place for bear traders.

Divergences are handy tools for both forex traders and technical analysts. However, every indicator or strategy they use is not entirely perfect. Many traders who had failures with divergences mentioned that they entered the trade way too early. Entering a trade soon can trigger stop losses and can end your trades prematurely.

**What to Look Out For:**
1. Make sure that you observe a crossover with the stochastic indicators in the technical chart. While trading divergences, you will often be tempted to enter into the trade without seeing a crossover. No matter how tempting it might be, always be patient and wait for the stochastic to cross over.
2. You can also use other trading strategies such as observing overbought or oversold conditions to check the momentum of the currency prices.
3. You can use trend lines on the indicators to observe the trend reversals if there are any. These tips can help you to stop entering the trade before.

# Rules for Trading Divergences

## *Rule 1:*

You need to find one of the below-mentioned chart patterns in the technical chart. If not, you are not observing a divergence pattern.

1. Double top
2. Double bottom

Also, always make sure that you observe higher highs or lower lows than the previous highs or lows.

*Rule 2:*

When you have got a sufficient understanding of divergences, you can now draw on them to make the next tops and bottoms. This higher-high and flat high can be used as bearish divergence, whereas lower low and flat low can be used as a bullish divergence.

Make sure that you draw a trend line using these divergence indicators.

*Rule 3:*

You can connect to higher peaks in the uptrend or two lower peaks in the downtrend. This can potentially mean that a divergence trend is happening.

*Rule 4:*

Make sure that you are constantly analyzing the price factors while drawing the trend lines with the divergences. Whether it is a top or bottom, you are connecting with both MACD or stochastic indicators.

You can use other indicators at this moment to increase the probability of your prediction becoming right.

*Rule 5:*

Always make sure that you are observing the slopes that are happening during the trade. This can help you to appreciate the importance of flattened prices in the technical analysis charts.

# Chapter 7: Binary Options

Binary options trading strategy has recently been in the news for controversial reasons. Many countries made it illegal to mention that binary options strategy as gambling. While there are reasons to believe this claim because the market is filled with untrustworthy market brokers, the strategy itself is not a scam. In this chapter, we will discuss the binary options strategy related to forex currency pairs. Follow along!

## What are Binary Options?

The principle of the binary options strategy is straightforward and self-explanatory. Binary options trading provides a way to bet on the market in the short term. Unlike stock markets or traditional options, what traders need to do is predict whether the price of a commodity or a forex pair will be either up or below the current market price. If a forex trader believes that the market price will be above the current market price, he will choose a call option. If a trader believes that the market price will be below the current market price, he will choose a put option.

You should have observed the risk associated with binary options by now. When you trade with binary options, you will have only two options. You either win or lose. While this can be technically called gambling, you should remember that you are predicting the prices of commodities or forex pairs but with a short time frame and a 50-50 probability.

## Where to Trade Binary Options

The problem with binary options trading is that it is unregulated, and this makes many fake brokerage scams spamming with advertisements and taking out profits by manipulating the market prices. So before trading with binary options, do smart research about the brokerage firm that you are willing to participate with your trades. There are more than a dozen reliable binary options trading platforms in the market right now.

With binary options, you can bet the prices of commodities, forex pairs, and some of the popular stocks. However, remember that binary options only provide trading options for major currency pairs in the forex market. Some of the popular forex pairs used in the binary options market are EUR/USD, GBP/USD, USD/JPY, and AUD/NZD.

# Binary Options Strategies

To succeed in binary options, you need to understand the risks that binary options come with. Many traders compare binary options with sports betting due to their volatile and unpredictable nature. Even the most successful binary traders win only either 60% or 70% of the trades. This fact makes us realize that following a strict strategy is essential for success with binary options.

*What do we need before starting?*

**Technical Analysis:**
As almost 90% of the binary options depend on short-term price fluctuations, you need solid knowledge about different technical analysis indicators. It is also essential to know a lot of known patterns for predicting the market movement efficiently.

**Fundamental Analysis:**
While it is true that fundamentals are not so crucial as technical indicators for trading binary options, you still need to make sure that you use them whenever needed. For example, price fluctuations happen due to a new economy or earning reports. Carefully following these fundamentals can help you to predict market movements. Remember that there you can also use long-term binary options if you want to dive in.

*Why is Having a Strategy Important?*

An excellent binary options strategy will help you to decide at what moment you need to start trading. Like any trading strategy, you need to calculate the opportunities and risks that a binary options trade may come with. Novice traders usually fail with binary options because they do not follow a strict strategy to climb the success ladder in the long term. A good strategy always has three main components:

1. **A trading strategy:** With a trading strategy, you decide what to do by following the principles such as value investing and strike rate. For example, a successful trader usually considers 60% as a reasonable strike rate.
2. **Risk management strategy:** Risk is inevitable in any trade. As a binary options trader, you are capable of losing your capital with just one trade if you want to. No one wants to lose money consistently, and not to make this happen to have a risk management strategy is very important.
3. **Analysis and improvement strategy:** We all learn by our own mistakes and experiences. Therefore, whenever you participate in binary options trading, ensure that you are journaling the results for future trades.

# Popular Binary Options Strategies

In this section, we will discuss some of the popular strategies that binary traders use. Of course, all these strategies can be used with major currency pairs in the currency market. However, you can apply these same principles to other financial instruments such as commodities and stocks.

### *The Best Strategy For Binary Options Traders*

Binary options forex trading is a wild world, and it involves much planning to win the race. This section has provided an approach that can help binary options traders effectively trade forex pairs.

**You Need to Find the Right Indicators**

As a trader, you need to find the technical indicators that can help you predict the movement of prices within the short term. Unfortunately, not all indicators can help you to identify signals that can help us to predict the movement.

Understanding support-resistance lines, moving averages, and oscillator signals can help binary options traders. In addition, knowing about different candlestick patterns can be a further advantage.

## You Need to Find the Right Time

With a basket of indicators, you now need the right time to observe them. So make small intervals and observe them accordingly. Usually a five minute period can be a reasonable time frame for binary options traders. However, swing traders can extend their timeframe to ten minutes to observe swing patterns while trading forex pairs with binary options.

Understanding reversal patterns can help you effectively understand the time frame analysis required for consistent successful trades.

## Finding the Right Trade Type

They are usually different types of trade types in a binary options market. The most popular are high/low options which can also be called call/put binary options.

Binary options traders can also utilize specific other trades as mentioned below.

### One-Touch Options

You need to predict whether or not the forex pair will touch a particular price. Traders will still earn money if the price decreases after reaching the price.

### Ladder Options

Ladder options are risky binary options with a high reward. You need to predict whether or not the forex price will reach two specific prices. Many experienced traders use ladder options as it offers a high return of investment

### Boundary Options

In this trade, you need to provide a boundary for the forex price. If the price remains in the boundary by the end of the trade, then you will win the trade.

### *One-Minute Binary Options Strategy*

In this strategy, you will place your trade for 60 seconds. At the end of the 60 seconds, if the asset moves according to your prediction, then you will receive profits, or otherwise, you will lose your profit.

## How Do We Effectively Place Trends for a 60-second Time Frame?

All you need to know is about support-resistance levels and how you can use them to predict the market movement. Support and resistance levels occur due to the pulling up of prices between bears and bulls. By correlating them with Fibonacci and pivot systems, you can effectively estimate whether or not prices will go up or down within the next 60 seconds.

When a trader participates in a one-minute binary strategy, he usually makes a bunch of these trades so that he can reach his strike rate of profits. Therefore, even though support and resistance levels are crucial for extremely short-term strategies, it is better to include price action and momentum analysis in your strategy for better profits.

*Momentum Strategy*

To be successful in binary options, you need to predict in which way the market is moving and find a way to predict with how much speed that the prices are either rising or decreasing. The calculation of momentum can only be possible by having a good grip of moving averages and historical price charts of that particular forex currency.

## What to Do in a Momentum Strategy:

Before trading binary options using a momentum strategy, you need to start using momentum indicator and boundary options. Using boundary options, you can list out two prices for the asset price to move, and if the price stays in between, then the trade is successful. However, the liquidity with boundary options is usually less, and thus you can only use it with major currency pairs such as USD/EUR.

The momentum necessary for this strategy can be calculated in three different ways.

1. **Absolute:** In this technique, the momentum will be calculated by comparing the present price movement with a particular price movement in the past. Traders use various technical analysis techniques to find out some reliable times where the market rallied in the same way.
2. **Process Oriented:** In this technique, traders take periods and price changes to calculate the momentum of the asset price. This process is more technical and involves a lot of mathematical calculations.
3. **Relative:** Using this technique, traders can estimate momentum by calculating the historical averages. It is a low-risk alternative but can only work with small market movements.

## 5-Minute Trading Strategy

The 5-minute binary options strategy is one of the more popular ones that traders often use. Five minute binary options strategy provides flexibility that the shorter time frame strategies do not give. With a five minute strategy, you can also make more than 50 trades per day if you want to with more success rate as you will have significant time to analyze the price movements.

Most traders use the money flow index (MFI) to predict the supply and demand that can influence the movement of prices in five minutes. However, fundamental analysis is not required for short-term trades as it is difficult to predict the changes using those factors.

Traders and trading platforms usually represent MFI from 0-100. Thus, it represents different scenarios that binary options traders can use.

1. If, for example, the value of MFI reaches either 0 or 100, it means that everyone is either buying or selling their positions.
2. When MFI crosses 80, it means that the forex pair is overbought, and it will fall anytime soon. Similarly, if MFI reaches 20, then the forex pair is oversold, and it will rise anytime soon.

Along with MFI, you can also use news trading techniques to predict the market movement in a 5-minute strategy. You, however, need to follow reliable paid subscription services to scrap the news data for you.

## Understanding Rainbow Strategy

Rainbow strategy implements a complex technical analysis principle known as moving average to predict the market movement. It is proven and is called a reliable strategy by many binary options traders.

In this strategy, traders will observe the crossover of three moving averages. Traders also use moving averages for shorter periods instead of longer ones as the longer ones take more time to appear in the technical charts.

You can use more moving averages if you want to, but the accuracy does not change. The rainbow strategy specifically recommends you use three moving averages. To work this strategy, you need to find moving averages that are both closest and fastest compared to the current price.

**What to Do**

Spot the three fastest and closest moving averages and point them to three different colors. Furthermore, now you need to observe these three moving averages for close to five minutes:

1. If you find that the medium moving average is above the shortest moving average it means that the prices are falling, and you need to take a put binary option.
2. If you find that the medium moving average is below the shortest moving average, the prices of forex pairs are rising, and you need to take a call binary option.
3. Some binary options traders check for 2 to 3 periods (usually 5 minutes) before jumping in the trade. However, you should not spend too much time as the accuracy will decrease after three periods.

*End of the Day Strategy*

This binary options strategy is more straightforward and uses fundamental analysis factors instead of technical analysis factors. The market is filled with different types of traders, and day traders occupy a large chunk. Day traders usually close their positions overnight, and they mostly do it at the end of the day.

Binary options traders use this principle and will trade only during the end of the day when there is less noise from swing or position traders. In this strategy, traders will observe closing gaps and determine how the market will move.

1. If the closing gaps are pointing upwards, then binary traders with forex pairs should consider a put option.
2. If the closing gaps are pointing downwards, then binary traders with forex pairs should consider a call option.

**Which Timings Should Forex Traders Use?**

Remember that binary options will only be available in the U.S. timings as it gets more market volume during these times. Therefore, unlike the forex market, which is available for 24 hours, binary options trading can be done only in U.S. market timings.

*Understanding Robot Strategy*

Trading binary options are entirely technical and lead to a lot of ups and downs. Additionally, not everyone has the time or psychological willpower to conduct binary options trading. Due to this reason, many forex traders consider using robots as a way to trade their binary options.

We, however, recommend you to manage your trades by yourself. However, if you want to spend your time in the real forex market and want to use binary options to create a passive income, then robot services that can analyze the market prices for you using various indicators and will make the trades for you is a better option. First do thorough research about the services before investing in them.

*Long Term Binary Strategy*

Binary options also provide a way for investors to look forward to predicting the prices in the long term. Traders who are efficient in fundamental analysis usually use this strategy to gain some profits over the long term. Six months or a year is usually a reasonable time frame for long-term binary options investors.

## What Should You Do?
1. Research about the long term growth of the forex pair you are willing to invest in.
2. Make sure that you verified all the fundamental analysis factors mentioned in the previous chapters.
3. Remember that you will lose all your money if you bet in the wrong direction. So, reconfirm your prediction using mathematical models or formulas for precision. You can use different strategies such as ladder options, boundary options, and one-touch options while trading in the long term.

*Understanding Volume Strategy*

Usually, traders ignore the impact of volume trends in the change of the forex exchange rates. You can combine volume trends with technical indicators to predict binary options effectively. Volume indicator shows how much trade is going on related to a particular forex pair.

If a lot of selling is going on, then the volume of forex pairs will decrease, and if a lot of buying is going on, then the volume of forex pairs will increase. Binary options traders need to closely monitor these volume trends and decide whether the trades are speculative or manipulative. For example, many big players use a bearish strategy to decrease the price of the exchange rates so that they can buy back at lower prices.

**What to Observe:**

1. High volume means many have already bought the shares, and there are very few traders remaining to buy the currency pairs. So, in the next period, a decrease in the currency will happen.
2. Less volume means traders have gone bearish and have liquidated their open positions. Many traders are looking forward to increasing the value of their open positions, and thus, the transaction value of the currency will increase.

*Understanding Breakout Strategy*

In any financial market, there will be a change from an upward trend to a downward trend. The exact position when an upward trend becomes a downward or a downward trend becomes an upward is known as a breakout. Binary options traders can utilize these breakout indicators to predict the movement of the forex pair.

**What to Confirm**

Use trend lines to conform to either an uptrend or a downtrend in the market. If the trade line then starts moving in the opposite direction, then the breakout has happened. Next, make a put or call binary option according to the opposite direction the value of the forex pair is moving.

# Chapter 8: Success In Forex Trading

Even though being the largest financial market globally, forex trading is not an investment route that many roots for. Only 10% of the traders succeed in the forex market, and 90% end up losing their money. While the above statement may seem demotivating for beginners, it is a fact that you can't escape from. To succeed in forex trading, you need to be technically sound and psychologically aware of the difficulties that forex traders need to face.

## Why Do People Enjoy Trading?

Trading is an adrenaline rush to many. Irrespective of the financial institution they are a part of, traders are passionate about what they are doing. However, while earning money and gaining profits should be one of your goals, they should not solely make you move forward in the market. Like any career, trading can be enjoyed only if you can understand its true essence.

## Why Is Trading Tough?

Traders have a hard job. Traders can gain money quickly and can lose all of it at the same time. This can lead to a lot of pressure on them, and the only way they can become sane is by controlling their emotions. Many successful traders remain patient, relaxed and will not lose their calm when the market moves opposite to their expectations.

## Why Do Forex Traders Lose Money?

Forex traders lose money due to various reasons. Journaling your trades and analyzing them carefully can help you find out the reasons for losing money trading. We will be talking about some of the reasons that make most forex traders lose money.

### Revenge Trading

Revenge trading happens when a trade of your expectations goes wrong, and you trade more money in an attempt to get back the money you lost. Revenge trading is a problem even for many experienced traders. Most traders can't accept the mistakes they have made or the crucial points or reports they have left out while doing fundamental or technical analysis.

To escape from revenge trading, you need first to accept that you are not going to win every time in the market. The forex market is unpredictable, and sometimes even rigorous research can not help you not fall from the ship.

### Greed and Fear

Greed and fear are both directly responsible for a trader's performance in the market. Greed makes traders be easily manipulated by big players in the market, whereas fear makes traders lose their capital quickly. It is evident that to be a successful forex trader, you need to be as rational as possible and should not let greed or fear dominate your decision-making skills.

Learning meditation, yoga, or participating in Neuro Emotional Technique (NET) can help individuals to control these basic emotions.

### Lack of Knowledge

For a forex trader, hunting for the necessary knowledge should be an essential skill. However, many traders ignore this fact and start to invest their capital in the forex market without any research or sufficient knowledge. We suggest you read magazines and trade journals, and attend both webinars and seminars to increase your understanding of how the market functions.

*Not Knowing How to Utilize the Capital*

Many forex traders make trades that they either can't afford or that will cover their losses because of high margin trading. While both leverage and margin trading are boons for a retail trader with less capital, they can be devastating if there are losses. You can lose your money sooner than you could imagine.

# How to Succeed in Forex Trading

Like every trading methodology, an individual can master forex trading and succeed in most trades by following a strict plan according to their research. Making a plan and following them even during high market volatility is what regular forex traders do with ease.

*Master Yourself for the Race*

Knowledge is an essential factor that can help you recognize popular trends and good entry/exit points during forex trading. Reading different case studies, magazines, trade journals, and real-life experiences from forex traders can help you to make a strategic plan for your trades.

*Differentiate Yourself Between Risk and Discipline*

Most of the traders fall under two categories. First, successful traders follow strict discipline and will not deviate from their plan. They are optimists and believe that their fundamental analysis can help them reach their successful path.

On the other hand, some pessimists always find excitement in participating in risky trades; they give both excitement and hefty profits. A perfect trader can find a balance between these risk and discipline factors. To succeed, make sure that you have discipline but also the commitment to participate in risky trades.

### Independent Decision Making

The internet is filled with gurus, masters, and influencers trying to tell you what you want to do. A successful trader never blindly follows this advice but will do complete research and absorb a lot of material before participating in a trade. Independent decision-making skills are an essential psychological skill for any trader irrespective of the financial market for success.

### Will Try to Know Their Negatives

Every trader has weaknesses. Some can't quickly grasp the technical indicators, whereas others cannot effectively analyze the reports. Make sure that you understand what your negatives are and try to improve them over time. Knowing your edge can help you in the long run.

### Deciding the Time to Trade

Forex trading is done 24 hours a day for six days a week. A beginner will always be confused when choosing a time horizon they can trade. It will be a disaster if you decide to make trades during different time zones. Having consistent timing while trading is essential for both professional and personal happiness.

Do your complete research and decide whether you want to trade during Pacific/ European/U.S. timings. Being the highest liquid market globally, there is always a lot of trade that goes on each of these timezones.

### Gut Versus Head

Traders often go through a war between their head and their gut before making a trade. Specifically, the head is when you thoroughly analyze trade and decide to go with the logic before executing the trade. On the other hand, the gut is what you think about this trade based on your past experiences, fears, and intuitive skills.

Choosing between your head or your gut, especially while trading, is a challenging task. As a beginner, we suggest you follow your logic and analysis during the initial trades. And over time, when you learn from your mistakes, we suggest you start believing in your gut more. There is no winner but a tie because both are essential for success.

# Importance of Having a Trading Plan

Planning is essential, especially if you are keen to make it a lifestyle. As a forex trader, you need to create your personalized plan instead of listening to experts. Every trader is on their own in this game, and your preferences, market views, and risk tolerance levels will help you make a plan that will work better for you. Having a trading plan can help you to minimize losses and gain profits over the long term. In addition, a trading plan will help you realize whether or not you are moving in the right direction. Remember that having a perfect plan cannot guarantee success. It will, however, definitely help you to cut out your losses.

To effectively follow your plan, you need to have trade discipline. The primary objective of trade discipline is not to deviate from the plan unless it moves towards drastic results.

### *The Best Approach for Forex Trading*

As a forex trader, you need to create your own strategic plan based on your currency pairs and the portfolio that you have already. You can also use derivatives such as options and futures to manage your risk.

While there are many ways to strategize your plan, it is better to learn about the inverted pyramid model, which is recommended to be used by beginners for starting better.

The inverted pyramid model is a classic way to strategize your plan in the forex market. It includes both fundamental and technical analysis to be done before executing the trade.

The basic idea is while using an inverted pyramid model, you first need to select a currency pair and revalue all the factors mentioned below to judge whether or not your currency pair is a better choice for trading or a long-term investment. Here are the different stages in this model for you:

1. **Macro Overview:** In the first factor, you need to judge the value of a currency based on international views. Consider whether any black swan events such as wars or terrorist attacks can happen. Then, understand the impact of international politics on the currency. All the factors need to be mega trends and should impact at least some parts of the world. For example, the impact of the Covid-19 pandemic can be considered as a macro overview.

2. **Market specifics:** In the second stage of the plan, you need to start researching what the market is thinking about the currency. You need to understand the impact of currency in the future from both speculator and central bank's perspective. Market specifics sometimes will also be correlated with political news. It would help if you also judged the market sentiment using various fundamental analysis factors described in the previous chapter of this book.

3. **Understand Indicators and Predict Price Changes:** Now you need to start to focus on indicators that can impact the exchange trade of the currency. First, analyze its performance with different currency pairs. Then, predict whether or not volatility can occur.

4. **Dig into Technicals:** For any trade, you must follow some of the technical indicators that can help you understand the present market sentiment for the currency. In addition, watching technical patterns constantly can also help you understand the behavioural mechanism of different types of traders in the market.

5. **Micro indicators:** Many fundamental and technical indicators affect the price changes. Many investors do not care, thinking that these will not make an impact. But understanding a set of these indicators and using them while trading can help them make effective entry and exit positions. Traders can also use stochastic indicators for a better understanding of the forex currency market.

# Brokers in Forex Trading

For success in forex trading, a good broker is essential. Unlike in the old days, we are now connected globally via the internet, which makes forex trading easy for retail investors. Previously only banks and financial institutions used to have the equipment to speculate the market's movement effectively. Now, you can do everything they do with a simple mouse click.

*Who Are Brokers?*

Brokers are the intermediaries to exchange your currency pairs or derivatives with others in the forex market. Being the largest financial market in the world, there are no liquidity problems for popular currency pairs. Choosing a good brokerage firm is essential, especially during a busy trading day.

*How to Choose Your Broker*

To choose a broker, you need to cross-check various technical details about the firm. Choosing a broker is a big step for your financial career. Unlike stock market brokers, there are only a few reliable brokers in the forex market. We have provided some of the factors that you may need to consider while choosing a broker.

### High Reliability and 100% Uptime

It used to be very difficult in the 90s to trade forex due to high transaction costs. Only after the internet became popular did online brokers start to emerge.

Usually, there are two types of brokers—dealing desk broker and no dealing desk broker. Dealing desk brokers take the two sides of the trade, whereas no dealing desk broker's act as a mediator between two traders.

If you are a day trader or scalper, we suggest you go with dealing desk brokers as they take tighter spreads and low commissions. However, it is more logical to go with a no dealing desk broker if you are a swing or position trader.

### Security

Before considering a broker, you need to ensure that they provide high-security standards for their clients. For example, a forex trading platform should have 2-factor authentication features to protect your account and have advanced security standards such as encryption mechanisms to secure you from brute force attacks.

Choosing a broker is a challenging task, especially if you are new to the market. Many brokerage firms are now providing their services with low commission rates. As a trader, you need to make sure that the broker is favourable with all mentioned below factors.

### Regulatory Compliance

All the brokerage firms in the U.S. need to be a member of the National Futures Association (NFA). So before starting an account in a firm, make sure you cross-check their name on the NFA website. It also should support the Certified Trust and Financial Advisor (CFTA) regulation for being a trusted brokerage firm for forex trading.

### Leverage and Margin

Forex traders need to focus mainly on leverage and margin requirements before selecting the broker. Leverage helps you to trade with more money than your capital. The margin amount is the minimum amount that the brokers need you to deposit to start trading.

Many brokerage firms right now are offering 200:1 leverage. Ensure you completely understand the concept of leverage before trading, as it can quickly drain your account balance.

### Commissions

Brokerage firms charge commissions for every single trade you make. So make sure that the commission fee is reasonable. Usually, forex brokerage firms charge commissions depending on the spread of the transaction. Here, spread refers to the difference between the bid and ask price.

### Deposit and Withdrawal Features

Make sure that the brokerage firm supports seamless deposit and withdrawal features. Taking a long time to deposit or withdraw your funds can be frustrating, especially during a busy trading day.

### Beautiful User Interface

The user interface has now become a mandatory feature for any trading platform. Take a quick look at how the website and apps are designed for the broker. Having a clean and neat UI can help you trade quickly.

### Customer Service

Not all are technologically savvy, and everyone needs assistance at some point in their trading times. Make sure that your brokerage firm provides both text and voice customer care assistance for you.

### Availability of Currency Pairs

Not all brokerage firms provide all currency pairs that are available in the forex market. Therefore, if you are essentially interested in trading with cross currency pairs, you should check out all the firm's currency pairs.

**Derivatives**

Spot trading is the most common way to participate in the forex market. However, there is the derivative market that is a preferable way for some forex traders. If you are interested in trading options, futures, forwards, or swaps, you need to check whether or not your brokerage firm supports them.

# What is Required to Open a Forex Account?

Opening a forex account with a brokerage account is pretty straightforward nowadays. We have provided a checklist that is essential for opening an account below.

1. A government-issued photo ID
2. A bank account for withdrawing/depositing your funds
3. A verified phone number for two-factor authentication to protect your account
4. Your tax information

And that's it. You can start trading in the forex market once your account is verified.

# Chapter 9: Risk Management For A Forex Trader

Traders study many details about different trading strategies, philosophies and fundamental analysis tactics to choose their winner. However, many don't worry about risk management strategies that need to be mastered by a trader to take away profits and minimize losses effectively. The psychological tendency to not think about failures is why many traders are not efficient in risk management. As a forex trader, you need to understand that learning risk management strategies and effectively using them in your forex trades is as important as trade selection.

## What is Forex Risk Management?

Forex risk management helps you to minimize any losses that can occur during a forex trade. In addition, an effective plan of risk management strategies can help you gain profits over the long term.

### *What Are the Risks Associated With Forex Trading?*

As a forex trader, you will be affected by various risks in your trading period. Having a good grasp of fundamentals about the currency pair you are trading can help you to list down the potential risks in the trade way before the trade is started.

Some risks a forex trader can face are:

1. **Currency risk:** The prices of the currencies often fluctuate to and fro. Trading in a volatile market is risky to buy a foreign asset as it can decrease in value within less time.
2. **Liquidity risk:** While there is no problem with majors in liquidity, several cross currency pairs have a risk of liquidity. Almost 90% of the currency trades involve USD, and if you are trying to liquidate your position that does not involve USD, you may face some difficulty.
3. **Interest rates risk:** Forex traders usually pay or receive interest rates due to the rollover policy that forex markets use to keep currency flow possible. While interest rates are monitored by the central banks most of the time, there are

chances that volatility can decrease your profits or lead you to losses because of a drastic change in interest rates.

4. **Leverage risk:** Forex traders have a powerful option known as leverage to make their trades. Certain brokerage firms even offer a 400:1 leverage option for traders. Unfortunately, while this may seem tempting, it also means that you will quickly lose all your capital if you bet wrong about the market movement.

5. **Technological risks:** Right now, many forex traders entirely depend on online brokerage firms to maintain their forex account. In a perfect world, everything will be alright. However, in a world where cybersecurity hacks are very common, you have a risk of losing all your trading balance with a simple phishing mail.

6. **Risk of scams:** As being the largest financial market in the world, forex traders are often lured to scams.

# Five Risk Management Strategies For A Forex Trader

All these Risk management strategies mentioned in the below section are universal and can be used for any trade. An efficient risk management toolbox, however, depends on customized risk management strategies depending on your portfolio.

*Strategy 1: Learn Everything You Can*

Many investors deal with risks because they are financially illiterate about the threats that may occur because of a bad trade decision in the forex market. With high leverage options available many traders are now dealing with much money and can lose them very soon if they are wrong with their predictions.

To succeed in this wild forex market and not fall at risk, all investors need to be aware of all the currencies, their economies, and the fundamental analysis factors that can affect their exchange rates. So make sure that you closely follow the economic and political details about major currencies.

It would be best if you also started to extend your knowledge about fundamentals and technical indicators to judge the risk of a particular position.

## *Strategy 2: Do Not Misuse leverage*

Yes, leverage is a boon for forex traders because it lets you play with the money that you do not own in the market. However, remember that while leverage is tempting, it still has its flaws. For example, all the brokerage firms right now are offering a 100:1 leverage option, and this can make traders become too involved in high capital trades which can cause them to lose their margin at a much quicker rate.

We will discuss position sizing in further sections and make sure that you understand the leverage risks and minimize them effectively as a forex trader.

## *Strategy 3: Effectively Using Stops and Limits*

Stop losses and limits are very complex tools that forex traders need to use in their every trade. Usually, forex traders choose stop losses that end prematurely. It would be best if you used stop orders and limits together to act as a better risk management system.

Take profits is also essential if you are worried about losing your profits due to constant market fluctuations.

## *Strategy 4: Use Risk - Reward Ratio*

You can use your capital and create a risk-reward ratio that can help you understand what you expect from the trade. Usually, as a forex trader, you need to target a 3:1 risk-reward ratio. It means that for a 50 USD loss, you are looking at a trade that can make you 150 USD per trade.

However, it is not so easy to find trades that can always give you a 3:1 profit. So, you need to be constantly aware of the trends and adjust your time frames, positions, and leverage options according to the risk-reward ratio you choose to follow.

*Strategy 5: Learn with Paper Trading*

As a beginner, you need to be aware of paper trading to test your skills as a forex trader. Paper trading works with virtual currency and makes you try various technical analysis strategies before implementing them in the real market.

However, the emotions involved with real trading are a whole lot different, and we suggest you use paper trading only for learning about risks that you may encounter in your trading journey.

# Understanding Position Sizing

The advantages of leverage are equal to the disadvantages it provides. To counter these disadvantages and minimize the losses, a forex trader needs to follow advanced risk management techniques such as position sizing.

*What Is Position Sizing?*

Position sizing stands for trading the number of units that you can trade without losing all your money at once. Thus, position sizing helps forex traders to stay in the game for a long time.

**How to Determine Your Position Size**

There are different factors that you need to consider before determining the position size for your trading account.

1. The total balance in your trading account.
2. The currency pair that you chose to trade. Is it a major currency or a counter currency?
3. How much of the money in the account are you willing to risk?
4. Did you place any stop losses or limits for the trades?
5. How is the exchange rate right now for your currency pair?

Usually, forex traders use a 1% or 2% position sizing. You can find yours using the factor mentioned above by any online calculator.

**Example:**

If you have 1,000 USD in your account with a 100:1 leverage, you can trade 100,000 USD in the forex market. With a position size of 1%, you can only risk with 10 USD that is 1,000 USD in the leveraged amount. However, you cannot continue this further because if you face losses consistently, your margin amount will decrease fast.

Understanding position sizing and limiting your trades with a strict 1% or 2% rule can help you tremendously in the long term.

# Using Stop Losses Effectively

All forex traders should know and understand the importance of stop losses. They can not only help you to end the trade automatically, but can also help you to understand how to avoid risks and gain profits over time effectively. All position, swing, and day traders use stop losses in their trading strategy. There are different ways to utilize a stop loss as a forex trader for risk management.

### *Use Stop Loss Based on a Percentage*

Let us suppose that you are willing to risk 4% of your account money for a single trade. Many forex traders use this percentage to set up their stop losses. However, it is a bad trade practice.

When we are talking about using percentages, we are talking about the arbitrary price movements in the market. Always consider the current market price and place a stop loss based on the risk level you are willing to jump into.

## *Using Support Resistance Level*

All forex traders use charts, and when they use charts, they specifically point out the support resistance level because it is an important factor to determine the momentum of currency prices. Therefore, as a trader, when you observe support resistance levels, you should not place your stop losses close to this boundary.

If you place a stop loss close to the support-resistance level, your trade will prematurely end, resulting in a loss for you.

**What to Do:**
1. Find the support-resistance line and create a boundary to determine the range they cannot usually fall to. Make sure that it is not too far from your strike price.
2. Place limits and stop losses to minimize further losses due to a sudden change in the support resistance level.

## *Using Market Volatility*

Volatility is common in the forex market. Many big players liquidate or buy currency pairs to stabilize the exchange rates or gain profits. Knowing the volatility and the factors that can identify volatility is important to set a stop loss.

Use strategies such as Bollinger Bands and average true range indicator to the range where volatility can occur.

## *Stop-Loss Based on Time Limits*

You can place stop losses based on a predetermined time. This works well if you are worried about high volatility during a release of a report by the government or because of being an intraday trader who needs to exit the trade by the end of the day.

Also, remember not to place stop losses in close ranges because they are of no use. Placing the stop losses so far away from the market sentiment is also not considered a good strategy. Instead, use both market forecast and market sentiment to determine the range of stop losses.

# Understanding Currency Correlation

As a forex trader, you need to be aware of the concept of correlation. Let us take, for example, the correlation between AUD and NZD. These currencies are closely linked to each other as they depend highly on each other.

When AUD falls, NZD will also fall. When AUD rises, the exchange rate of NZD will also rise. Many major currency pairs in the market correlate, and as a forex trader, you need to understand its principles to manage your risk effectively.

### *How to Measure the Correlation Between Currencies*

To help traders estimate the correlation between different currencies, the forex market has introduced the correlation coefficient. It usually ranges between -1 and +1. Plus one represents that the currency pairs are highly related, whereas -1 represents that the currency pairs are not correlated. The correlation of currencies is usually represented in forex tables.

### How to Not Fall Prey to Correlation:

1. Never invest in currency pairs that are correlated. If you do this, you will be doing overexposure, resulting in losing all your amount when the currencies move opposite your prediction.
2. It is not counterproductive, so please diversify all the currency pairs you are trading. Make sure that they have a correlation coefficient of less than zero.

However, remember that many factors affect the correlation of currencies. For example, Brexit has made the correlation between GBP and EUR decrease. You need to be both politically and economically knowledgeable to understand the correlation between currencies. Complete thorough research and use this as a risk management strategy for your portfolio.

# Conclusion

Forex trading is fun, exciting when you are winning, and devastating when you are losing. This book has provided basics, various strategies, and different philosophies to predict the price movements for a beginner. Technically there are a lot of other things that you can master further to understand market trends, fundamental policies, liquidity, and volatility. This final chapter is designed to help you know some of the tips, techniques, and psychological traits that a forex trader needs to develop to lead a happy professional life.

## Seven Important Tips to Remember as a Forex Trader

### Do Not Trade Out of Boredom

In the forex market, price changes are often slow, and huge price fluctuations happen only once in a while. This slow dynamic change of prices results in traders participating in different random trades without any solid research. These random trades can affect your portfolio and can make you lose profits over time. Therefore, never trade without research, analysis, and commitment.

### Problems with Overtrading

Trading is addictive and often results in an obsession with the game more than with the money. Unfortunately, many traders face the overtrading problem, which can affect your future and ruin your personal life.

To escape from overtrading problems, start to use stop loss and take profits whenever needed. Make a rule at the start of every day, and do not let yourself deviate from this quota for the day even when you are at a loss. It would help to restrict your trading time to a specific time zone and for specific days.

*Facing with Slumps*

Any trader who has been in the market for more than one year will understand that slumps are common in the market. Forex traders are said to have only 55% of successful trades in a year. That leads to 45% of the time where you will be frustrated, devastated, and let down because of your bad predictions.

Everyone has their way of dealing with slumps. Some will reduce their trading volume, whereas others will take a break and return when they feel right to trade again. Slumps can lead to revenge trading and sometimes to bet the market with huge leverage.

Here are some best strategies to follow during a losing streak:

1. **Square up:** By squaring up, you will be liquidating all of your existing positions not to face further losses. While some recommend holding the positions, it is recommended to square up when you have lost your confidence due to the losing streak.
2. **Trade less than the usual:** It is better to reduce your day trading volume to at least 20% of the usual for focusing on things more precisely. Cutting down position size can increase your confidence when there are profits and can make you do a reality check when there are losses.
3. **Share your failures:** There is nothing better than confessing your mistakes to the trading community. There are many news boards, blogs, and forums to let forex traders share their experiences with the market. However, if you are not comfortable sharing your strategies with the world, we suggest you talk in front of a mirror about the trades and the strategies you have followed.
4. **Take a break and research:** If your decision-making skills are affected by the losses, it is better to take a small break and have a short vacation or your own time with your family. Remember that taking a big break can make you lose your consistent approach to the market. Come back soon as you can to start trading.

You can also spend your time researching different currencies, commodities, and economies to approach your next trades. Taking some time for research and retrospecting your approaches is a good trading skill.

*Happiness*

As a trader, you need to find ways that can make you happy. Usually, traders go through a stressful job, and being motivated and happy can help them in the long term. You need to treat trading just like any profession, even if you are doing it part-time. Love trading and it will give you happiness and financial independence.

*Do Not Constantly Check Out the Market*

Traders often have a problem of constantly checking the market updates while trading in an open position. While it is true that you need to work during trading hours, the problem with forex trading is that it runs 24 hours, and constantly checking it without strict timings can make you overwhelmed and can also affect your personal life. So stick to a time and check your position's performance only during this time.

*Eat and Exercise*

Personal health and hygiene are extremely important for the success of a forex trader. Make sure that you are living a healthy lifestyle. Exercising and doing yoga or meditation can help you to control your emotions while trading. Exercise can also be a good deviating factor from the mental stress that traders face.

*Enjoy Trading*

Is it hard to enjoy trading? Maybe yes and maybe no. However, many professional traders declare that they enjoy the process no matter how stressful and devastating it is. Enjoying trading is essential, especially if you want to do it for a long time.

# Importance of Trading Journal

Maintaining a trading journal is essential if you are looking forward to making a future or for securing your position as a trader in the market. Journaling can help you introspect, learn from your mistakes, and can trigger ideas from experience. We are not necessarily asking you to follow the traditional paper-pen system to make your trading journal. Right now, there are tons of digital software for traders to help them journal their trades effectively.

Trading journals make you disciplined, patient, and help you generate your philosophy that can help you make crucial decisions in future trades. Trading is a learning process, and what is better than learning from your own experiences, victories, and debacles?

Trading journals also provide how far you have progressed since you have started the forex journey. They help you remember your landmarks and trades that made you understand the wonders of the forex market.

### *What Should I Write in My Trade Journal?*

Journaling is a personal preference, and everyone has their way of mentioning the details that matter to them. However, we have provided some information to help you make it a better tool for your trading career.

### Motivation for the Trade
Write detailed information about the motivations that made you go forward with the trade. For example, attach news reports or magazine sources that triggered you to trade that particular currency pair.

### Market Views and Philosophy
Provide information about what the market views are about that currency pair at that particular time. Also, mention the trading philosophy that you have chosen to go forward in the trade.

### Observations
Mention all the observations that you have learned after the trade started. You can attach charts, reports in this section for better introspection in the future.

### Mistakes
When the trade ended in the wrong way than you anticipated, it helps if you note down all the mistakes in the trade. Then, in the future, skimming through your mistakes can help you not repeat them.

**Statistics of Performance**

After the trade ends, mention the statistics such as profits or losses along with the Prove/ Loss ratio. In addition, it will help if you can mention the reasons for your success or failure in the trade along with your score from 1 to 10.

# Forex Trading Scams

Being the largest financial market in the world, the forex market has become an easy way to pawn forex traders by scamsters. While most of these scams will cease over time, many beginners still get lured to their false claims of heavy returns. The National Futures Association is trying hard to notice these scams and inform the traders. Therefore, make sure that you verify the authenticity of a forex service or broker before investing your money.

## *How to Identify Scams*

Complex computer algorithms are now automating many scams to manipulate the spread call prices and generate a share with the trade. Few other scams such as signal sellers are used to manipulate an investor's mind by saying that they will receive guaranteed returns when they provide capital to them. Once they collect from investors, they disappear, and it will be hard to track them.

In recent days, robot scams have also become extremely popular in the market. Individuals are approaching traders with software that can automate the trades and guarantee a good return on investment. No matter how great their algorithms are, it is never a good idea to bet your portfolio on automatic trading software.

Here is a checklist to avoid yourself from scams:

- Do good research before investing.
- Ask for suggestions in forums or bulletin boards. Ensure that you ask these doubts in a trusted community because these scamsters can act like normal people to remain authentic.
- Research about the founders and whether or not you can legally sue them if anything goes wrong.

- Do not believe in your gut while choosing a product or service related to the market. Always believe in logic, and if you are not ready, do not invest your money in it.

## Final Words

We are glad that you have reached the end of this book. Being a forex trader is an exciting job, and we hope you will utilize the techniques and strategies provided in this book to kick start your forex trading journey. We wish you all the best. Happy Trading!

Disclaimer:

All the details in this book are only for your educational purpose. The author of the book is in no way responsible for your trading decisions. Make sure you do Trading with only the money you can afford to lose. If you are still unaware, please contact a professional advisor regarding your trades.

# References

*9 Rules for Trading Divergences.* (2021, April 18). BabyPips.com. https://www.babypips.com/learn/forex/9-rules-for-trading-divergences

Bennett, J. (2019, August 12). *9 Things You Didn't Know About Successful Forex Traders in 2020.* Daily Price Action. https://dailypriceaction.com/blog/successful-forex-traders

Chen, J. (2019). *Learn About Trading FX with This Beginner's Guide to Forex Trading.* Investopedia. https://www.investopedia.com/articles/forex/11/why-trade-forex.asp

DailyFX. (n.d.). *Forex Fundamental Analysis.* Www.dailyfx.com. https://www.dailyfx.com/education/forex-fundamental-analysis

*Forex Technical Analysis | Learn Forex Trading| CMC Markets.* (n.d.). Www.cmcmarkets.com. https://www.cmcmarkets.com/en/learn-forex/forex-technical-analysis

*How to Succeed with Binary Options Trading at Home 2021.* (n.d.). Www.binaryoptions.net. https://www.binaryoptions.net/

Killian, A. (2020, June 30). *Top risk management strategies in forex trading.* IG. https://www.ig.com/en/trading-strategies/top-risk-management-strategies-in-forex-trading-200630

*The 7 Major Forex Currency Pairs in Trading | CMC Markets.* (n.d.). Www.cmcmarkets.com. https://www.cmcmarkets.com/en/trading-guides/forex-currency-pairs

TradingwithRayner. (2017). *Forex Risk Management and Position Sizing (The Complete Guide).* TradingwithRayner. https://www.tradingwithrayner.com/forex-risk-management/

*What is forex and how does it work?* (2019). IG. https://www.ig.com/en/forex/what-is-forex-and-how-does-it-work

Milton Keynes UK
Ingram Content Group UK Ltd.
UKHW031325270823
427563UK00021B/585

9 781087 889269